CHASING THE ENTERPRISE

Achieving *Star Trek*'s Vision
of the Human Future

SCOTT ROBINSON

ISBN 978-1548623258

Cover art by Jim Wampler / Mudpuppy Games
Author photograph by Elizabeth Castle Lane

Chapter headings font Final Frontier Old Style, and subheadings font Final Frontier, were created by Allen R. Walden

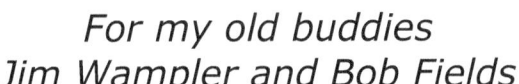

For my old buddies
Jim Wampler and Bob Fields

Also by Scott Robinson...

The author wishes to acknowledge
Dr. Jerald Hughes of the University of Texas
for his partnership in the development of the theory of
cognitive diversity presented herein.

Table of Contents

Prolog: September 1976

It's September 1976, and I'm a 15-year-old high school sophomore.

And *Star Trek* is five years younger, an uncelebrated decade old this month - though no one is yet noticing that sort of thing, this early in *Trek* history.

And Gene Roddenberry – the Great Bird of the Galaxy himself! – is coming to a civic arena near me.

My friends and I coerce a parent into driving us from Frankfort, Kentucky to Louisville's Freedom Hall, where we experience for the first time what we've only read about, up till now – Trek fandom, up close and personal. Those wonderful fan fests they'd had in New York, on the West Coast – we in the Midwest are now entering that amazing world for the first time!

Fans in homemade Starfleet uniforms.

Tables packed with *Trek* memorabilia for sale. I buy a poster.

A screening of a worn black-and-white print of "The Cage."

A screening of the infamous blooper reel.

And more than an hour of the Great Bird, pontificating on the future of - and the potential of – the human race.

Along the way, he serves up all his greatest hits from the college lecture circuit: how he fought to keep Spock in the cast for the second pilot; 'Letter from a Network Censor'; why he bailed on Season Three, all of it.

He talks about Questor[1], and his belief that technology will one day deliver us from our weak, frail meat bodies. And how *Star Trek* is a watered-down version of what he *really* believes the future will be like.

He doesn't talk about starships and Klingons and phasers, or even the cool tech awaiting us in the future – tricorders, transporters, warp drive. Oh, in passing, a bit, but that isn't his focus.

---

[1] Questor was the protagonist in Roddenberry's 1974 TV pilot *The Questor Tapes*, the last of a long line of androids planted on Earth to guide humanity to maturity.

His focus is *us*. Human beings – what we are, what we can be, what we are becoming. *Star Trek*, the glitzy nacelles of our imaginations, isn't the thing – it's just a hailing frequency for something much bigger, much grander, much more important.

I stand in line later that evening, clutching my overpriced poster, and I find myself in front of the man himself – imposing in stature, yet congenial – and shake his hand after he autographs my poster.

I'm a 15-year-old high school sophomore, and it will be years before I truly absorb and fully understand what I've seen. It will become more clear in the decade to come, as Roddenberry goes to war with Paramount and Harve Bennett and Nick Meyer, fighting for his humanistic vision as the *Trek* films unfold – and again as *The Next Generation* emerges, and the tussle over the vision of *Trek* begins anew.

Star Trek and I are now both past 50. Today, many of *Trek*'s tech dreams have already come true: we communicate, planet-wide, with little hand-held boxes; doctors can scan our insides with machines; we talk to computers and they talk back to us. But, again, that's not what *Trek* is really about.

Today, the contrast between Roddenberry's vision of the human future and the competing dystopias that choke our cable channels could not be more stark; his belief in humanity, the beings we can become stands out in high relief, a lone beacon, even as we in the real world keep tumbling back down the social incline with Sisyphean regularity.

And today, having had many years to ponder, we may wonder: can we really become what Gene Roddenberry imagined humankind to be?

"Star Trek was an attempt to say that humanity will reach maturity and wisdom on the day that it begins not just to tolerate, but take a special delight in differences in ideas and differences in life forms. If we cannot learn to actually enjoy those small differences, to take a positive delight in those small differences between our own kind, here on this planet, then we do not deserve to go out into space and meet the diversity that is almost certainly out there."

~Gene Roddenberry

"Our People Are Perfect..."

"We stress humanity, and this is done at considerable cost. We can't have a lot of dramatics that other shows get away with - promiscuity, greed, jealousy. None of those have a place in Star Trek.*"*

~Gene Roddenberry

Many are the reasons that *Star Trek* not only endures in our cultural consciousness fifty years on, but continues to renew itself each decade. Many are the influences it wrought not only on our culture, but on our technology, our emerging global perspective and our personal journeys. Many are the echoes of its many voices, from the original holy trinity of Kirk, Spock and McCoy to Picard and Riker and Data and Troi, Captains Sisko and Janeway and Archer, the many dozens of voices surrounding them, in stories that will live within us forever.

At the center of it all, we find that the deep pull of *Star Trek*, holding its fans securely through the years, is a core concept, a single idea, a powerful message emanating through every incarnation, through endless obstacles and obfuscations: Humankind is approaching the end of its adolescence; the future is optimistic,
bright, hopeful, a place of peace and social prosperity, a haven of challenge and achievement and fulfillment.

These ideas are not unique to *Star Trek*, of course; but few and far between are the books/movies/series that go as far as *Trek* and its creator in painting human destiny as ultimately positive.

"I believe in humanity," Roddenberry once said. "We are an incredible species. We're still just a child creature, we're still being nasty to each other. And all children go through those phases. We're growing up, we're moving into adolescence now. When we grow up - man, we're going to be something!"

Philosopher, junior grade

It didn't really begin that way. The evolution of *Star Trek* is well-documented, and its original incarnation wasn't explicitly a humanist statement; Roddenberry hadn't yet gotten there.

But it was on its way. Once the show made it onto the air, its commitment to ethnic diversity was already in place: though the man in the middle was a white male American, he was surrounded by an Asian, a Bantu woman, a Scot, an American southerner – and, of course, an alien, with a Russian soon to join[2].

Roddenberry had even tried to introduce a little feminism, making the first officer of the Enterprise a woman in the original pilot. In his telling, the network pushed back at a woman in authority, and told him he could have either the female first officer or the alien, but he couldn't have both.

But while Roddenberry hadn't yet discovered humanism or begun integrating it into his creation, he nonetheless had the seeds of it beginning to sprout in his mind.

The earliest significant example was "The City on the Edge of Forever," written by Harlan Ellison, a first-season episode still considered by most to be the finest *Star Trek* story ever, five decades on. Ellison's original script featured Enterprise crewmembers dealing drugs and even killing other crewmembers – and Roddenberry was having none of it[3]. He insisted Ellison rewrite it, eliminating the criminal element. Ellison did, but not to Roddenberry's satisfaction. Roddenberry then had two staffers rewrite it, then rewrote it himself. Ellison was livid, and remained so for decades.

"I was told [the criminal crewmember] was nixed because no one on board the starship *Enterprise* could be a bad guy," Ellison wrote in a 1975 essay. "I railed at that concept. It always struck me as nonsense that the network could try to pass off a space battle-cruiser of that size, with a complement of many hundreds of people, without a few rotten apples in the barrel."

High standards among his starship crew, however, did not a humanist utopia make. The full bloom of humanism in Roddenberry's thinking was yet to come.

---

[2] It should be noted that the character of Chekov, a proud Russian nationalist, was added at the height of the Cold War.

[3] The entire story is told in Ellison's book *The City on the Edge of Forever: The Original Teleplay That Became the Classic Episode*, White Wolf, 1994, which features his original script.

Humanism: any system or mode of thought
or action in which human interests, values,
and dignity predominate; a variety of
ethical theory and practice that emphasizes
reason, scientific inquiry, and human
fulfillment in the natural world and often
rejects the importance of belief in God.

It was, in fact, after the cancellation of the original series in 1969, in correspondence with Isaac Asimov that Roddenberry was exposed to humanism as a philosophy. Asimov, a humanist crusader for much of his five-decade career as one of science fiction's leading authors, had written a book about the Bible[4] from a purely atheist, scholarly perspective. He sent a copy to Roddenberry and initiated a discussion of humanism and what it stood for. Asimov, an icon among humanists and one of its leading expositors, cultivated Roddenberry as a humanist evangelist – with *Star Trek* as his pulpit.

Star Trek and humanism were made for each other. In *Star Trek*, humanism not only had its ideal crucible – a society with an energy-rich economy, a vast expanse of cultures and intelligences (fictional, but analogically representative of real human nations), new and unprecedented human potential for discovery, exploration, and growth – it had built-in validation in Roddenberry's multinational crew and institutions (Starfleet, the Federation) dedicated to peace.

All of this didn't dawn on Roddenberry all at once. As the Seventies got underway and his efforts to create something new for television failed again and again[5], he found financial relief on the college circuit, where *Star Trek*'s growing popularity in syndication led to large, enthusiastic crowds wherever the Great Bird was speaking. These talks, sampled on a 12" album called *Inside Star Trek*[6] , included Roddenberry's anecdotes about his years making the show; his battles with the network, humorous stories, insights into the creative process – and large dollops of decidedly humanist philosophy, which firmly took hold in the growing *Trek* fandom's collective consciousness. Roddenberry became known as much for his humanist meanderings as for his godlike status

---

[4] *Asimov's Guide to the Bible*, Random House, 1969.

[5] Roddenberry's follow-up series attempts included *Genesis II, Planet Earth, The Questor Tapes* and *Spectre*.

[6] *Inside Star Trek*, Columbia Records, 1976.

as *Star Trek*'s creator. He began referring to himself as a "philosopher, junior grade."

And the junior-grade philosopher wasn't content to simply haul water for Asimov's actual humanist institutions; not only did the *Trek* future feature peace, an end to poverty, and a dedication to human well-being – it boasted the eradication of *all* human weaknesses. In the *Trek* future, Roddenberry came to expound, there would be no more conflict *at all* – no more greed, no more jealousy, no more pettiness, no more racism, no more misogyny.

"That developed between the first *Star Trek* and the second *Star Trek*," said Maurice Hurley, writer/producer on *Star Trek: The Next Generation*[7].

A decade after Roddenberry's ascent into humanism – and two decades after the original series – *Star Trek* returned to television, and Roddenberry had a chance to coalesce his humanist thinking into an ordered *Star Trek* universe, one that would proselytize for the futuristic philosophy for which he had now become known.

"In the 1970s, people started saying that Gene was a visionary, when he had this utopian vision of the future," said *TNG* writer Ron Moore. "I think he started to believe that, and then *Next Generation* became a vehicle to demonstrate this utopia."

Retroactively, a fiction evolved in which Gene Roddenberry had conceived *Star Trek* as a humanist document from Day One – but that wasn't true.

Wacky-doodle Gene

When Roddenberry returned to television in 1986 to begin developing *Star Trek: The Next Generation* for Paramount, his humanist reputation was now steering his thoughts and plans for his resuscitated creation. In many ways, this was not only natural but conceptually essential: all of *Star Trek* that followed – four more television series and eight more feature films – settled into the Roddenberry vision.

But as *Star Trek* prepared to leave dock again in the Eighties, it wasn't that simple.

"[Gene's] emphasis on an optimistic future wasn't new," wrote Roddenberry biographer Joel Engel[8], "and it, too, was writ overly large by a man with a lot of money, an aversion to Judeo-Christian beliefs, and few

---

[7] In William Shatner's documentary *Chaos on the Bridge*, 2015.

[8] *Gene Roddenberry: The Myth and the Man Behind Star Trek*, Hyperion, 1994.

inhibitions. Not only would the future be peaceful, it would be virtually utopian: members of the Federation, [Gene] posited, have evolved to the point where they no longer conflict with each other, because conflict itself is obsolete."

"Gene's ideas about the future, and about man, are wacky-doodle," said Hurley, who became *ST:TNG*'s de facto show runner in its second year. Caught between the urgency of keeping the rickety new series afloat and Roddenberry's humanist dreams, he found himself defending stories about people he just couldn't believe in.

"The research prior to *The Next Generation* led him to have a thesis that... man was evolving in a humanist way,[9]" was how William Shatner put it.

"[Gene] sees us now in our infancy," Hurley said, putting it less politely, "where we just gather and accumulate like a three-year-old in a crib, *That's mine! That's mine! Gimme this! You can't have that! I need this! I need that!*"

"He believed that mankind in the 24th century had resolved all conflict between themselves,"[10] said Rick Berman, who by 1990 had become Roddenberry's successor. "Most science fiction that we experience today is a relatively dismal view of what the future's going to be like. Gene was obsessed with the idea that the future was going to be better."

"Gene's conception on *NextGen* is almost heavenly," said *TNG* writer Brannon Braga, "in that everyone's at peace."

All of this took the form of constraints upon *TNG*'s writing staff. The central characters of the show were not to be in conflict with one another; they were to be expressions of Roddenberry's humanist vision, cooperative and harmonious and at peace with one another.

This did not go down well.

"Some writers chafed against Gene's vision of a better future where there was no conflict," said Braga. "It takes away everything you need for drama!" Hurley railed.

"If you tell a writer that the characters can't have conflict between them," Berman added, "you're just cutting his legs off."

Dorothy Fontana, recruited from the original *Trek* alumni to write for the show and serve as story editor, also weighed in: "If our people are perfect, and have no problems or conflicts between them, there is no story here."[11]

---

[9] *Chaos on the Bridge.*

[10] Ibid.

[11] Ibid.

"We would walk around into each other's offices going, 'I don't know how to write about that. I don't know how to write about perfect people'"[12] said *TNG* writer Melinda Snodgrass. "The essence of drama is conflict."

"The dictums gave the writers a lot of stress and struggle, and then, in most cases, Gene would just take the scripts, and he would just rewrite them," Berman said. "And these writers were not used to that, and it was very, very frustrating, and a lot of writers left." David Gerrold, possibly the most famous *Trek* writer among fans and, like Dorothy Fontana, an old guard recruit for the new show, ballparked the writer/staffer turnover in the first season alone at 30[13].

"That was Gene's vision of *Star Trek: The Next Generation*, take it or leave it, and work within it or don't," said Braga, who took the rules as a personal challenge. "I liked the dramatic constraints that it put on me as a writer. I had to find new ways to tell stories."

In the end, Roddenberry's superhumanistic rules of All Peace, No Conflict prevailed, when incoming producer Michael Piller changed the dynamic of the show in the third season. The plot-driven stories of the first two years gave way to character-driven drama, where each week was a Picard story, or a Data story, or a Worf story – and the conflict was generally with outside characters, dilemmas, threats, and situations: Klingons, Nausicans, Ferengi, and other characters not of the enlightened Federation.

This even brought about the development of two new and long-standing *Trek* personae – the omnipotent, godlike trickster Q (created by Roddenberry), and the Borg (created by Hurley), cybernetic hive beings bent on assimilating all others. As existential threats, they provided not only plenty of conflict but allowed the writers to explore fascinating themes.

Though the next three *Trek* series would provide workarounds for the No Conflict rule – *DS9* was based on a multicultural outpost; *Voyager* featured a hybrid crew of Starfleet and its political opponents; *Enterprise* takes place not in the 24th century but the 22nd, before humanity's enlightenment – Berman, as guarantor of Roddenberry's vision, strove to remain faithful:

"I think he really believed in this positive vision of what mankind was capable of," he said. "I subscribed to that idea all throughout all the different shows that we did, because I felt I owed that to Gene."

---

[12] Ibid.

[13] Ibid.

An Undiscovered Country

It was just before his death that Roddenberry confronted the most powerful and sustained affront to his vision.

That affront came from Nicholas Meyer, who arrived in *Star Trek* after Roddenberry's disastrous 1979 attempt to bring *Trek* to the cinema – *Star Trek: The Motion Picture*. Bloated, overpriced and just plain dull, *ST:TMP* was every bit the humanist manifesto had been building toward through the Seventies. It was also flat, unexciting, and slow.

Roddenberry was benched by Paramount, with producer Harve Bennett taking over and Nicholas Meyer handling the directing and the script[14]. Meyer, the most bona fide intellectual in the *Star Trek* universe, brought Shakespearean gravitas to the task, his strong literary cred guiding both his scripting and staging choices. His take on *Trek* promised to be both exciting and brainy.

And it was. *Star Trek II: The Wrath of Khan* (1982) is still regarded, thirteen films in, as the best of the *Trek* movies. Meyer achieved it largely by discarding Roddenberry's input: the Meyer Enterprise was a militaristic place, filled with human frailty and conflict, no trace of humanism to be found. He and Roddenberry agreed on only one premise: that Captain James T. Kirk reflected the character of the classic seafaring Horatio Hornblower, an idea that appealed a great deal to the very literary Meyer.

Fast-forward nine years, more than three seasons into *TNG*, to the sixth *Star Trek* movie, also directed and co-written by Meyer. With Leonard Nimoy as executive producer and co-conspirator, Meyer contrived a story about "the [Berlin] Wall coming down in outer space," a parable of current events at the time. *Star Trek: The Undiscovered Country* found the aging crew of the Enterprise on one final mission – détente with the Klingons, now struggling for economic survival after a cataclysmic accident.

Within Meyer's story, the crew of the *Enterprise* – and Kirk in particular – must confront the prejudice they feel for their lifelong enemies, as a Klingon chancellor makes a bid for peace and cooperation with the Federation. A conspiracy between Starfleet officers, Klingon commanders and Romulan politicians complicates Kirk's bumpy journey toward closure and reconciliation.

---

[14] Meyer's only previous big-screen credit was *Time After Time* (1979), an unusual sci-fi film about H.G. Welles and Jack the Ripper, though he had distinguished himself earlier with *The Seven Percent Solution*, a best-selling Sherlock Holmes novel.

In short, the story was Meyer's now tried-and-true recipe for *Star Trek* success – and filled with everything Roddenberry hated.

As the film's production got underway, Meyer and his team met with an ailing Roddenberry, who as executive consultant was in the habit of reviewing scripts and giving notes.

It didn't go well.

"This is… a movie about prejudice," Meyer said at the time. "And as such, Gene Roddenberry had a lot of difficulty with the script, because he believed, very strongly, that in the future where *Star Trek* takes place, there would be no prejudice. And I, taking a somewhat darker view, pressed ahead, with the notion that there is no evidence for the diminution of prejudice."

Meyer made the movie he wanted to make. It was a success – debuting a mere two weeks after the death of the man who started it all.

In his autobiography[15], Meyer recalled the confrontation:

"I suppose underneath it all was a conviction on my part that Roddenberry's was a specious utopian vision for which there was no historical evidence," he wrote. "Did he really believe in the perfectibility of man, or (as I suspected[16]) was it just some sort of pose? I was cynical, maybe because somewhere along the line, I'd learned that Frank Capra was a Republican. I found myself straining against the shape of the *Star Trek* bottle, rewriting the words of the Mass, not merely altering the music. These were big no-no's, but I mulishly persisted, straying off the Federation reservation and not caring whether I ever found my way back to the Neutral Zone. Against Roddenberry's complaints, I dug in my heels. Where was there any evidence, I wanted to know, that bigotry had disappeared - or would disappear - in human affairs? Was racism still not a powerful force in America? Were the Serbs and Croats not intent on 'ethnic cleansing'? Were not Muslims still fighting Christians? Had it not always been thus since the beginning of man? What, I demanded, was the justification for Roddenberry's optimism? The evidence of millennia was on my side. In the meantime, I insisted, in my movie people would continue to act like human beings."

---

[15] *The View from the Bridge: Memories of Star Trek and a Life in Hollywood*, Viking, 2009

[16] Meyer's questioning of Roddenberry's sincerity of vision is answered by a comment from *TNG* producer Robert Lewin: "I was convinced Gene really lived in the 24th century," he said. "It was in his head day and night. There wasn't a question you could ask him about the 24th century that he didn't have an answer to. Many times I would hear him say, 'They would not do this in the 24th century… things are different than that."

Meyer later expressed regret over the manner in which he had treated Roddenberry in that final meeting. He never, however, relented in his opposition to Roddenberry's vision of the human future.

"Roddenberry really believed in the perfectibility of man, of humans, and I have yet to see the evidence for this," he told the *LA Times* in 2011. "In fact, in his original *Star Trek* concept, there wasn't any conflict. So he always had problems with writers who were trying to write conflict, because that's what drama is."

Family Feud

As this book goes to press, *Star Trek* is poised to return to television after a 12-year absence. *Star Trek: Discovery* will debut in the fall of 2017.

Nicholas Meyer is one of its writer/producers.

Another is Rod Roddenberry, Gene Roddenberry's son.

In other words, a new *Trek* series is about to debut, helmed by two men with opposing interpretations of Roddenberry's universe.

On the one hand, there is Roddenberry's vision of a peaceful humanity, dedicated to our collective success and eventual victory over our personal frailties and social dysfunction. On the other, there is the Meyer view, that there is no evidence that such an evolution is possible.

Meyer is wrong.

Though the evidence of the past 10,000 years does indeed support his premise that Roddenberry's humanist vision is well out of reach, the evidence of the previous 290,000 says the opposite.

Not only can we become the species Roddenberry wanted us to be, in the distant past – we already achieved it.

"Star Trek points to a future in which human civilization is advanced enough to provide everyone with the basic necessities of life. It also shows us the ways in which we have already achieved that society, even if we have not decided to make it available to all… As technology progressively eradicates the need for labor, will we cling to Han Solo, to individual toil and competition motivated by material want? Or will we bend … the 'terrible arc of the political' toward something resembling collective freedom?"

~ Manu Saadia

A Tale of Two Franchises

Star Wars, Star Trek, and Macroeconomic Theory

Silicon Valley venture capitalist Peter Thiel, in a conversation with *New York Times* columnist Maureen Dowd, weighed in on that most famous of geek controversies: *Star Wars or Star Trek?*

Though rich, powerful and at least nominally conservative, Thiel is most qualified to join this particular fray. Though he hasn't been spotted at many West Coast Comic-Cons, he nonetheless can claim geek cred by way of his investment choices: he pals around with Elon Musk and Mark Zuckerberg. Thiel himself might not pass for geek, but he loves to fund it.

The interview drew the attention of Manu Saadia, who wrote the book *Trekonomics: The Economics of Star Trek*, which we will be discussing in this book more than once. Writing for *The New Yorker*, Saadia took note of Thiel's fanboy preference – *Star Wars* – and took note of his reason why.

"Capitalism," he answered.

"The whole plot of *Star Wars* starts with Han Solo having this debt that he owes, and so the plot in *Star Wars* is driven by money.

"*Star Trek*," on the other hand, "is the communist one."

Put simply, *Star Wars* appeals to Thiel's more libertarian sensibilities, while *Star Trek* evokes the horrors of a capitalism-free universe with lots of equality, no poverty, and completely egalitarian opportunity. In an essay published by the Cato Institute, he wrote that technology is often a dangerous distraction to social attention; freedom, he wrote, is a product of political thought, not technological advancement. And *Star Trek* seems to say the opposite.

Star Wars "is in fact much closer to home that *Star Trek*," Saadia wrote in *The New Yorker*. "Forget the lightsabers and the Force: the essential story of the films is familiar, a techified version of a Wild West that existed only in Buffalo Bill's travelling revue and its celluloid successors, the Westerns. In *Star Wars*, criminal potentates hire bounty hunters to recover debts from roguish smugglers. Robots are menial servants and sycophants rather than colleagues, and human slavery persists. Unelected tyrants and religious zealots make policy by fiat. A blaster, or a Death Star, is the only real guarantor of life and liberty. Fate and the lottery of birth reign supreme. It is a libertarian's fever dream, a distilled expression of the idea that the greater good is best served through unfettered (and, if necessary, brutal) economic competition.

"This, rather than the liberal-democratic setting of the USS Enterprise, is the political environment in which Thiel seems to feel most comfortable...in [his Cato Institute essay] he places 'confiscatory taxes, totalitarian collectives, and the ideology of the inevitability of the death of every individual' in opposition to 'authentic human freedom.' Only the strong and lucky, like Han Solo, should survive."

On the other hand, in the *Star Trek* universe, "technological progress is inseparable from society and politics," Saadia wrote. "As even quasi-fans will recall, the TV shows and films feature a machine called the replicator, which can produce any inanimate matter on demand – food, drink, warp-drive parts...The replicator solves, albeit fictionally, what John Maynard Keynes once called 'the economic question' – that is, the imbalance between supply and demand, and the resulting need for markets and price mechanisms to allocate scarce resources. The society of *Star Trek* has decided not to exact a fee for the use of the machine. Thus the replicator can be an engine both for the equal distribution of wealth and for personal enrichment. It does not bring about social change on its own. The post-scarcity world in *Star Trek* is the result of a political decision, not of pure technological progress."

It's an interesting new take on a very old debate: *Star Wars* as a 'libertarian fever dream,' *Star Trek* as the ultimate 'liberal-democratic' ideal. Yet it's spot-on accurate as sociopolitical characterization, when we consider the feudal mythologies that inspired George Lucas and the contemporary philosophy behind Gene Roddenberry's overt humanist manifesto.

In the *Star Wars* universe, life is cheap and freedom precious, because it's in such short supply. Authoritarianism reigns, in constant tension with the rage of the oppressed, with survival-of-the-fittest as the rule – and technology is leveraged only to serve this dynamic, never to rise above it.

In the *Star Trek* universe, life is revered and freedom the default, in bountiful supply. Egalitarianism reigns, and the right of self-determination is the highest rule. Technology is leveraged in its service, overtly bolstering equality, rather than enabling its antithesis.

This leads us to a fun and very interesting question: what, exactly, is the difference in these two universes, this opposing visions of human socioeconomic order?

The *Star Wars*-Wild West analogy might lead us astray here. It seeks to situate Han Solo, Luke Skywalker and company in a resource-sparse economy, where smugglers thrive, moisture farmers eek out a living wringing water from the air, and energy is flat-out hard to come by. Poverty is always within shouting distance, and human beings are used as beasts of labor.

Star Trek, on the other hand, shows us a society built on an energy-rich economy, where no one goes hungry, every living being is respected and nurtured by the society, and boundless accomplishment is possible.

It is easily argued that free and plentiful energy is the key difference between these two socioeconomic models.

But that argument is just as easily dismissed. In the *Star Wars* universe, all weapons – *even swords* – are energy-based; ships that are orders of magnitude more massive than the USS Enterprise roam the stars; planets can be blown to pieces. If anything, the *Star Wars* economy is *more* energy-rich than *Star Trek*'s.

We're looking, then, not at technology, nor even at energy supply, to pin down the critical difference in these two economies. And Peter Thiel's attitudes, per Saadia's essay, underscore it:

> "What is anathema to Thiel in *Star Trek* is the notion,
> drawn from Isaac Asimov's fiction, that the market is but
> a temporary solution to imbalances in supply and
> demand, and that technology and plenty will eventually
> make it obsolete. *Star Trek* replicators are nothing but
> Asimov's robots disguised as coffee machines, let loose
> on the world as a public good. They dissolve the need for
> a pricing mechanism. They represent the logical
> endpoint of the Industrial Revolution, when all human
> labor has been offloaded to machines. *Star Trek* and
> Asimov remind us that the market and all the behaviors
> associated with it are temporary and historically
> contingent. If that is so, then what Thiel thinks of human
> nature and motivations – that people are competitive,
> acquisitive, greedy – is temporary and contingent, too."

And there we have it.

Star Wars and *Star Trek* are not simply two very different visions of human society. They are two very different – and competing – views of human *nature*.

Are human beings competitive, acquisitive, greedy? That's an easy argument to make.

The follow-up questions are not so easy: have we always been so? And are we necessarily so?

Star Wars says Yes.

Star Trek says No.

"I think if we all lived in my Star Trek *world, it would be pretty close to heaven."*

~Gene Roddenberry

"Unclouded vision ahead requires that you deal with what is. To deal with what is, you must free your forebrain of your personal value system and personal preferences. You must discard all - or at least most - of your prejudices. Not just simple intolerance about race, religion, and so on. It is much more difficult than that. You must free your mind of those values dearest of all to you: affection for your home, your background, your country, its customs, your own culture, your religious beliefs. The more precious the belief to you, the more certainly it must go if you are to free your forebrain to use its perception and logic. Some very able and intelligent people are unable to endure this exercise, even for a few hours. Some people get angry at even the suggestion that they drop all their preferences. Almost a castration complex - "I can't give that up!" At a recent conference, someone asked, "Why go to all that trouble? Why not just read some good books about the future?" Which falls into the category of questions you wish that pleasant, intelligent-looking people didn't ask. Aside from the not-inconsiderable advantages of learning to free your forebrain to do what it was clearly designed to do, I shudder at the thought of anyone making a trip as important and perilous as tomorrow while totally depending on someone else's vision."

~Gene Roddenberry university lecture, quoted by Yvonne Fern in Gene Roddenberry: The Last Conversations

Tomorrow is Yesterday

Can we really become what Gene Roddenberry imagined humankind to someday be? Is the humanist vision of *Star Trek* achievable in the real world?

Nick Meyer and a host of former *Trek* writers say No. Peter Thiel not only says No, but that the *Trek* future is a thing to be avoided.

It is certainly not a trivial question. At this writing, in 2017, the world not only doesn't seem to be headed in the right direction, it appears to be going the other way entirely. In the United States, an authoritarian has been elected president; LGBT rights, which made tremendous gains over the past few years, are headed for rollback; education, voting rights and poverty-fighting social programs are on the chopping block. International tensions are rising, and both militarization and police powers are on the rise. The environment is increasingly at risk, and a healthy economy is about to be retooled to cater to the greed of oligarchs.

It's easy to look at the world as it is in the early 21st century, gaze ahead to the 23rd, and believe we just can't get there from here.

But we certainly can. And we *know* we can. How do we know? Because we've already been there…

All Our Yesterdays:

The Real Human Past

The Flintstonization
of the Human Adventure

If hope for Roddenberry's humanist future is found in the past, then our first task is to review and reevaluate that past, to search for clues about human nature that might support that hope.

And right away, we run into trouble. As it turns out, most of what people think they know about human prehistory turns out to be wrong.

There are lots of reasons for this. To begin with, the serious study of human prehistory is a very recent thing. The first pre-Sapiens fossils – fragments of a Neanderthal skull in Belgium - were only discovered less than 200 years ago. The age of the earth was just established in the 1950s, and the decoding of the human genome was only achieved in the past 15 years.

In that time, many myths about "cavemen" have made their way into the public consciousness – through the media, the movies, popular books – and even cartoons.

In their groundbreaking 2011 book *Sex at Dawn*, Christopher Ryan and Cacilda Jethá faced a similar barrage of myth. Gathering together the most recent research into the evolution of human sexuality, they noticed that even the most reputable scientists sometimes display a tendency to think about the distant past in contemporary terms – to allow passive assumptions to distort the review of evidence and the development of objective conclusions. They called this tendency "Flintstonization."

"Just as the Flintstones were the 'modern stone-age family,'" they wrote, "contemporary scientific specialization concerning prehistoric human life is often distorted by assumptions that *seem* to make perfect sense. But these assumptions can lead us far from the path to truth...All too often, we inadvertently weave our own experiences into the fabric of prehistory."

This tendency has two major causes, they continued, "a lack of solid data and the psychological need to explain, justify, and celebrate one's own life and times." They noted that several great thinkers of the past had exalted modern humankind by calling forth speculative images of a brutish human past – Thomas Hobbes, Jean-Jacques Rousseau and Thomas Malthus, specifically, each of whom used those images to justify his own portrait of an evolving human nature.

The result, they went on to claim, is a muddle of wrong-headed ideas in the public's understanding of prehistory, a compendium of myths that must be called out and replaced with facts, in order to arrive at a more accurate portrait.

The biggest myths are these:

- Early humans were "killer apes," savage and violent;
- They wandered the landscape in loose alliance, possessing little social organization;
- Females were fought over and treated as prizes by the males;
- They communicated by grunting and gesturing, and coerced cooperation through aggression;
- They were poverty-ridden and half-starving, barely scratching out an existence;
- It was every caveman for himself.

In clearing out these myths and getting to the reality, we begin to get a better picture of who we really are – and whether or not we can eventually measure up to Roddenberry's vision.

The Savage Curtain

Myth: Early humans were "killer apes," savage and violent...

"We admit that we're killers, but we're not going to kill...today! That's all it takes."
                    ~Kirk, in 'A Taste of Armageddon'

Most of us have *2001: A Space Odyssey* to thank for it, but wherever we may have picked it up, the Myth of the Caveman as Club-Wielding Brute is deeply entrenched in our cultural consciousness.

It's an iconic image, ironically committed to celluloid during the very months of *Star Trek*'s television debut: A wandering tribe of African australopithecines has a rumble with another tribe over a watering hole, and the pensive Moonwatcher, having noticed that the thigh bone of a dead boar makes a formidable extension of his own arm, proceeds to use that bone to club one of the opposing gang to death, thus committing the first murder. Flash-forward to 2001, and the image of an orbital nuclear warhead platform.

The image has stayed with us over the decades, augmented by a general cultural perception that it represents a real chunk of the human past: the idea that bloodthirsty violence was an evolutionary adaptation that got us where we are today, and that it informs our understanding of who we've come to be, a dozen years beyond 2001.

The inclination to turn in that direction for an explanation of the human condition, especially in the mid-twentieth century, is understandable: after two world wars and tens of millions of deaths, the default assumption that human beings are innately vicious, violent and homicidal is not a great leap. Years and years of violence-ridden evening news leaked it into the public gestalt.

Beat It with a Stick

We've seen variations of that message all over the place – in films, on television, in novels and comic books – and Arthur C. Clarke went out of his way to make it part of the human story he sketches out in *2001*. He was trying to make the story as factual as possible, and at the time, the idea of hominids as violent, murderous creatures represented the best thinking of anthropologists. Clarke got these ideas from author Robert Ardrey, whose popular books *African Genesis* and *The Territorial Imperative* had been best sellers.

Ardrey had, in turn, taken the notion from the work of Australian anatomist Raymond Dart, who had turned his mind to an interesting problem and come up with a solution that seemed to answer a number of questions about both our ancient past and our contentious present. The problem Dart tackled was explaining a pile of bones in South Africa, in a place called Makapansgat.

The Makapansgat dig was a cave containing a massive stockpile of humerus and femur bones – the long, thick, clunky ones within the upper arms and legs of mammals – and was faced with answering the question, why these bones and no others? Some of the bones were human; some were from gazelles, and so on. But beyond these, there were only fragments of other, smaller bones.

Dart's solution was elegant. The bones, he suggested, were weapons, and their cave stockpile was essentially an armory. The long, thick humerus and femur, regardless of source, make for a deadly extension of the human arm. Such a tool would confer an overwhelming advantage in a fight.

Building on this idea, Dart recast early humans as the brutes we see in our pop-culture myths: bloodthirsty killers and cannibals, ruling the African veldt as merciless packs of enraged hoodlums, cruising the savannah, spoiling for a fight. Ardrey spread this picture far and wide, all the way to Clarke, and what came to be known as the Killer Ape Theory – the idea that violence is a human default, a necessary step in our evolution – entered the public consciousness, where it remains today.

The problem is: well, it turns out not to be the case.

Cat Scratch Fever

Enter Charles Kimberlin Brain, known for some reason as "Bob," of the Transvaal Museum. Enthused by Dart's Killer Ape Theory and anxious to explore it, he sought out additional bone accumulations, similar to the one at Makapansgat. An expert in cave taphonomy (the study of environmental features and conditions), Brain was an ideal investigator to continue the work.

But what he found simply didn't fit Dart's story. In a project that stretched on year after year, as more and more specimens were examined, Brain found a pattern that turned the Dart profile of early humanity upside down: within the bone accumulation sites, those big bones – taken at first for clubs – were covered with scratches…from the teeth of large cats.

The stockpiles were what remained of leopard kills, over time, the largest bones being the only ones too large for the cat's jaw to break open for their protein-rich marrow. Fragments of human skulls, also too large for munching, were likewise found in the stockpiles – and likewise bore the teeth marks of big cats. Moreover, no other human artifacts were present, none of the stone tools used by hominids at the time, when they should have been, if the cave sites were in fact hominid habitats; and no stockpiles like the ones at Makapansgat have ever been found at a site of human habitation.

Dart's picture of human brute as apex predator, then, collapsed, not many years after *2001* was released in 1968, and the Killer Ape Theory has been discarded by anthropologists, for the most part. It was the big cats – the leopard, the saber tooth and their kin – who ruled Africa as apex predators.

Humankind, on its way to world dominance, remained prey in its prehistoric years. (As a footnote, Dart was delighted when he learned that his theory had been overturned, as any true scientist would be; and lest we view Brain's refutation as any sort of I-said-he-said, note that Brain spent 25 years at the task, examining well over a quarter of a million bones.)

Nor was *2001*'s image of the australopithecine Jets-Sharks rumble ever supported with anthropological evidence of intra-species warfare, or even battle between hominid competitors. If we have been beating each other's brains out with clubs for three million years, then Africa would be riddled with archeological digs of battlegrounds.

And we don't find them in Europe, where Cro-Magnon and Neandertal had their showdown far more recently. Instead, our cousins seem to have slipped away quietly, without fuss, left not upon battlegrounds but whole, within their homes.

Why does all of this matter? Because the Killer Ape Theory was disproven decades ago, yet we still see ourselves through that ghastly and disturbing filter. As well-meaning as Clarke and Kubrick (and countless other science-driven scenarists) may have been, we are still hauling around the self-image of the vicious savage, rather than that of the industrious survivor. Maybe we need a new movie, I don't know, but it's certainly time for a new narrative: one that cultivates the message, within our collective consciousness, that the murderous beasts among us are the exception, not the rule; and that we are, for the most part, determined and resourceful beings who lust not for blood, but for light.

Reality: Human beings were prey, not predator; survivalists, not killers...

"We lived as hunter-gatherers for 99-plus percent of our history as human beings. So our feelings, our specifically human feelings, have been shaped in that environment. But we're not living in that environment anymore; and in particular we're living in environments where population densities are probably a hundred times, much more than a hundred times, greater than they were. So we're having to interact in a much more complex way with a much larger number of people than we're really properly evolved to do. And so there are going to be some difficulties."

~Vincent Sarich, UC Berkeley

The Naked Time

Myth: Early humans wandered the landscape in loose alliance, possessing little social organization…

Crouching behind a rock formation on Taurus II, where the shuttlecraft Galileo has touched down, Spock and McCoy, along with astrophysicist Boma and security officer Gaetano hear a nearby group of large primates preparing to attack them.

"What do those super-sensitive ears make of that, Mr. Spock?" asks McCoy.

"Wood," Spock replies, "rubbing on some kind of leather."

"They're getting ready," says Gaetano. "They'll attack!"

"Not necessarily," Boma replies. "It could be a simple tribal rite, assuming a tribal culture."

"Not a tribal culture," Spock asserts. "Their artifacts are too primitive. More likely a loose association of some sort."

Spock's description of their Tauran predators mirrors the image that most of us have of early humankind – brutish, murderous, only vaguely connected to one another, let alone to us.

But whatever's out there on Taurus II, early humanity wasn't like that at all.

As discussed earlier, human beings were much more prey than predator in the millennia preceding civilization. Through the many stages of evolution that made us who we are, our brains grew larger and larger – a result of increased protein in our diet, metabolized at a lower energy cost when we discovered fire and learned to cook it.

And in our growing brains, expanding tissue and new components enabled us to capitalize on the innate cooperation we carried forward from our primate roots: the larger our brains grew, the more efficiently social we became as a species.

We learned to hunt more efficiently together than separately; to enhance our chances of survival through cooperative gathering and distribution of food; to share in the care and feeding of our young, distributing the labors of childrearing across our growing communities.

Rather than being the selfish opportunists a previous generation of anthropologists assumed us to be, we were socially sophisticated, optimizing our social brain power by jointly pursuing high standards of collaboration and mutual service and care.

The British psychologist Robin Dunbar put numbers to it. By studying communities of different species of primates (including humans), he discovered that there is a strong correlation between brain shape and volume, and the maximum social group size of a species - the greater the brain volume, the higher the community membership.

Put another way, our neocortex – the part of our brain that processes input from other human beings – can handle a certain number of social relationships. In our case, that number is roughly 150.

Based on this understanding of our social brains, we can begin to see a very different social framework emerging in our examination of our past. We weren't nasty and brutish, combative and disorganized: we were socially sophisticated, sharing the work load and its fruits, participating in the care of the young, looking after our elderly.

We made durable, effective tools for hunting, preparing food, and processing useful animal remnants like skin and bone for other purposes. Our knowledge of the available nutrition in our environment was exhaustive – many regions of Africa, where we persisted for almost 300,000 years, offered as many as 300 different edible plants.

We understood the signs of weather and even, to some degree, the meaning of the different positions of the moon and stars, relative to the seasons – essential for predicting approaching cold and the movement of edible animals.

We were efficient migrants, trucking large communities across long distances, following rivers and pitching tent in the right place at the right time to thrive on the megafauna that kept us well-fed.

We were, in a word, magnificent.

Across the spectrum of time, we achieved this sophistication at astonishing speed: while it took more than 70 million years for us to proceed from walking on four legs to two, it took a mere three million to make us the best hunters on Earth, and a final million to grow huge brains that set us apart from all the rest of creation.

Reality: Early humans were socially sophisticated, admirably well-organized.

A Private Little War

Myth: Warfare is a natural activity, as old as humanity...

"Well," says McCoy as Omicron Ceti III recedes on the bridge's main viewer, "that's the second time man's been thrown out of paradise."

"Maybe we weren't meant for paradise," Kirk answers. "Maybe we were meant to fight our way through, struggle, claw our way up, scratch for every inch of the way. Maybe we can't stroll to the music of the lute. We must march to the sound of drums."

If Kirk is right in this scene – if the martial impulse is inherent in human nature – then the prospects for Roddenberry's vision remain dim.

But the classic *Trek* canon gives us ample evidence that Kirk's fists-and-phasers-first tendencies, while prominent, were constantly tempered by Spock's calming rationality and McCoy's bottomless compassion. It wasn't about Kirk the individual, but Kirk/Spock/McCoy the team (and individual vs. group, a dynamic central to our thesis, will be explored later on).

This gives us a follow-up question to our previous chapter: If human beings aren't "killer apes," not predisposed to personal violence – might groups of humans still be inclined to collective violence? Is warfare part of our nature?

Winston Churchill thought so:

"The story of the human race is war. Except for brief and
precarious interludes, there has never been peace in the
world; and before history began, murderous strife
was universal and unending."

Much evidence can be mustered to support the first half of Churchill's
argument. As far back as written history goes, organized war has been with
us. But "before history began, murderous strife was universal and
unending" is a statement not supported by fact.

A growing body of evidence, however, is reinforcing the idea
that *Homo sapiens* is neither inherently violent nor warlike, that this has
always been the case, and that intra-species violence and organized conflict
are recent innovations for humanity.

Cemetery 117

Winston Churchill's famous assumption above is shared by many.
Recorded history shows no deficit of vicious physical conflict between
groups. The patriarchal religious texts of antiquity are bursting with tales
of deity-ordered slaughters and conquests; actual histories, all the way back
to the Sumerians, demonstrate patterns of almost constant warfare. The
assumption that human beings have not only engaged in organized
violence since the dawn of our species is not without impetus.

But saying that human beings are natural warmongers requires more
than supposition - what is the evidence?

We know from the fossil record what the violent death of a human
being looks like: a number of fossils - the Maba skull in South China, and
Cranium 17 from the Pit of Bones in Northern Spain, clearly show violent
death-by-handmade-weapon.

But that's not the same thing as organized warfare – one group of
humans planning and executing a homicidal attack upon another. We know
what that looks like, too, and it looks very different.

We see rare, isolated personal attacks – one-on-one – between
individual humans deep in the fossil record, reaching back to our pre-Cro-
Magnon predecessors; but we only find fossil evidence of actual warfare in
that period of time since the last ice age ended.

Jebel Sahaba

Jebel Sahaba – also known as Cemetery 117 – represents the oldest
evidence of organized human warfare found to date. Located in the Nile

Valley near the Sudan border, it contains more than 60 human skeletons, almost half of which died as a result of human violence.

Estimated to be over 12,000 years old, the Jebel Sahaba burial site was discovered in 1964 during the UNESCO High Dam Salvage Project, which sought to salvage archaeological sites in the path of the under-construction Aswan Dam. Led by Fred Wendorf, the site 117 team recovered numerous skeletons of men, women and children, 21 of which had stone projectiles in their bodies. Others had marks of their bones suggesting attack with sharp weapons – and some possessed previously-damaged bones, implying a violent culture predicating their cumulative ending.

The victims buried in Cemetery 117 are thought to be members of prehistoric Egypt's Qadan culture, a hunter-gatherer affiliation that persisted for an impressive 4,000 years. The Qadan were believed to have been organized enough to initiate an early form of farming, cultivating grass and grain for sustenance but lacking the knowledge and insight to do so in a structured fashion.

They also left behind sophisticated stone tooling, putting weapons of war firmly within their grasp. This, plus their ability to accumulate resources *en masse* - resources to be protected/plundered - indicate a people who had achieved the necessary ingredients for organized warfare – perhaps the very first ever do so. Cemetery 117 is the oldest evidence found to date of such a capability.

Nataruk: Bigger, Badder, Bloodier

If Cemetery 117 was the first incidence of organized warfare in prehistory, it was by no means the worst.

In 2012, west of Lake Turkana in Kenya, another mass grave was discovered. This one contained at least 27 different bodies, dated as having died between 9,500 and 10,500 years ago. Better preserved than the victims of Jebel Sahaba, they presented clear evidence of "to crania and cheekbones, broken hands, knees and ribs, arrow lesions to the neck, and stone projectile tips lodged in the skull and thorax of two men."[17]

The site, Nataruk, contained eight distinct males and females, as well as five other adults of indeterminate gender. Six children were in the grave. Four of the dead individuals were tied up, and one was a late-term pregnant woman.

"The injuries suffered by the people of Nataruk—men and women, pregnant or not, young and old—shock for their mercilessness," according

---

[17] M. Mirazón Lahr et al. 'Inter-group violence among early Holocene hunter-gatherers of West Turkana, Kenya', *Nature* (2016)

to Dr. Marta Mirazon Lahr of the University of Cambridge, principal investigator on the published study describing the site.

Unlike the Jebel Sahaba bodies, the Nataruk victims were not buried, as such: they were found in a depression that had once been a lagoon, into which they had been thrown.

The point is not the horror of these and other incidents we know of in our near prehistory: the point is that our near prehistory is the only time period in which they can be found. The human timeline is littered with the bones of those who walked it – but only in the past 13,000 years, since the end of the last ice age and the dawn of agriculture and permanent settlements, are we certain that such organized violence has occurred.

If violence between human tribes has been the norm throughout human history – if mass attacks, one group upon another, had been commonplace throughout the phases of the Paleolithic – there would be many such cemeteries. If, indeed, we inherited our homicidal impulses from the foreparent we share with the chimpanzee, as anthropologists insisted for half of the 20th century, then we would be finding not only mass graves of humans, but cemeteries filled with Neandertals, hominins erectus and habilis, and many of our cousins.

Unless and until such evidence surfaces, we are forced to conclude that our homicidal impulses are not innate, not built into our genes, but a learned aberration - and a very recent one, at that.

The Taste for Armageddon

A number of other ideas help to dispel the assumptions of Dart, Ardrey et al. One is anthropologist Raymond Kelly's observation that warfare is demonstrably not universal; studying indigenous societies that remain today yields a clean distinction between war-like and peaceful (an observation echoed by Jarod Diamond, Douglas Fry and others).

Kelly notes in his 2000 book *Warless Societies and the Origins of War* that warless societies tend to be *unsegmented*:

> "Unsegmented societies have a minimum degree of
> elaboration of internal or composite social groups; while
> segmented societies are internally demarcated e.g., into
> lineages, moieties or clans. No level of organization
> beyond the local community is found in unsegmented
> groups; while in segmented ones there are levels of
> organization bundled within the local community.
> Within local groups of unsegmented societies, families
> are usually identifiable as detachable constituent units;

while in segmented societies, within local groups, families are not identifiable as detachable constituent units, but are one segment in sa larger grouping. In unsegmented societies, nuclear families tend to predominate within the local group; while in unsegmented societies, nuclear families are only one form of family organization and corporate extended families are common. In unsegmented societies the culturally recognized coactive groups are limited to the family and local community; while in segmented societies, the culturally recognized coactive groups are limited to the family and local community; while in segmented societies, the culturally recognized coactive groups found are not limited to the family and local community. In unsegmented societies there are no units that are equivalent in structure and function. In unsegmented society there is no segmental organization and no segmental hierarchy; while in segmented societies there is both segmental organization and segmental hierarchy and segmental organization is a combination of like segments and progressively more inclusive groups within a segmentary hierarchy. Unsegmented groups show no corporations of any sort; while corporations are a common feature of segmented societies e.g., lineages and clans."

What causes societies to become segmented? Per Polish anthropologist Bronislaw Malinowski, the cause is surplus production: with the advent of agriculture, it became possible to store food, a development that certainly had its upside, but triggered the invention of politics and economics, which have pronounced downsides.

Kelly also notes that unsegmented societies demonstrably lack the concept of vengeance: group violence between clans does not exist because clans themselves do not exist; the concept of group liability cannot form, and so retaliation never occurs to anyone.

Finally, says Kelly, "it is evident that violence is not a unitary phenomenon and that the development of war entails the institutionalization of practices governed by a distinctive social logic that renders the killing of a killer's consociate a socially meaningful, morally appropriate, and emotionally gratifying form of reciprocation."

Anthropologist Augustín Fuentes added the following, in Douglas Fries' War, Peace, and Human Nature: "[Human warfare] is best seen as emergent from social structures, ecologies, and histories rather than being reflective of specific adaptive patterns of aggression and competition. It is not a basal human aggression that results in warfare or a basic human egalitarianism that results in peace. War and peace emerge from the interactions of patterns of cooperation, shared and disputed ecologies, social, economic, and symbolic histories, and the perceptions of human polities."

Reality: Warfare is a recent human invention, and is not a natural behavior.

"By studying the past, especially the more remote past of human origins, we can learn a lot about ourselves in terms of what it is that is special about humans, what it is that is in our nature, if we can get beyond projecting our own views of human nature onto the past (onto the Neandertals, among others), then hopefully we can learn something about what it is that is really part of being human and what of it is part of the very complex, and in many ways, very artificial world that we've created around ourselves..."

~Erik Trinkaus, University of New Mexico

What Are Little Girls Made Of?

Myth: Females were fought over and treated as prizes – as property - by males.

It is an arena in the mountains high above the Vulcan desert, outside the city of ShiKahr – Koon-ut-kal-if-fee, "the place of marriage and challenge." As Spock's relatives shuffle in, overseen by family matriarch T'Pau – the only person ever to turn down a seat on the Federation Council – McCoy is unsettled by the abundance of weapons. "In the distant past, Vulcans killed to win their mates," Kirk had explained earlier.

Spock's intended bride, T'Pring, invokes the kal-if-fee – the challenge – and chooses Kirk as her champion, committing him to a fight to the death with her lover Stonn.

"T'Pring, thee has chose the kal-if-fee, the challenge," T'Pau says. "Thee are prepared to become the property of the victor?"

"I am prepared," T'Pring responds.

Setting aside that T'Pau, an elderly woman, is perhaps the most powerful person on all of Vulcan, and is in charge of Spock's clan rituals, the exchange over the fate of T'Pring is an odd one. The winner of the upcoming battle will claim her as "property," indicating that Vulcan is distinctly patriarchal – which is, given T'Pau's station, illogical.

Yet we see the same dynamic between Spock's father Sarek and mother Amanda in "Journey to Babel," a dynamic he repeats with his second wife Perrin in *Star Trek: The Next Generation*: in Vulcan culture, the man is dominant, the woman submissive.

And the fact that in the past "Vulcan [men] killed to win their mates" underscores that the women were prizes to be won in battle – again, they are considered property.

Yet this backward and illogical state of affairs is simply a reflection of our own real-world myths about women and their role in the prehistoric past.

As far back as written human history goes, women have been subordinate to men. Our ancient religious texts show patriarchy as the default social frame, with detailed examples of explicit subordination of females. Historical records, epic poems, folklore and literature from cultures around the world, from every century, depict men in charge and women in service; and moreover, women are often portrayed as less intelligent, less civil in their behavior, and even "unclean," by arbitrary religious measures.

Even in our enlightened times, women in the United States only received the right to vote a century ago, and the privilege of owning a credit card independently in the early 1970s. We know, empirically, that the idea that human females are in any way inferior to males, intellectually or emotionally, is nonsense – yet, to a degree, the subjugation of females persists, and the cloud of social disdain toward women still hovers in many regions of the modern world.

The question to be answered is this: has it always been so? Has *Homo sapiens*, as a species, always experienced this social distinction between males and females?

The assumption of anthropologists and primatologists for more than a century was, yes, *Homo sapiens* and its hominin predecessors all lived within a social order that placed males above females, as seen in other primates – chimpanzees, most immediately, but also gorillas, gibbons, and others.

But that model has been challenged repeatedly in recent years, as evidence has arrived via anthropology, archaeology, paleontology, and even our decoding of the human genome.

Here's a broad array of that evidence, all in support of the reality that human females were the equals of males in prehistory, not their subordinates.

Chimpanzee culture as a model does not apply to Homo sapiens. In *Sex at Dawn*, Christopher Ryan and Cacilda Jethá methodically define the biological distinctions between our closest primate cousins, the chimpanzee and the bonobo.

The chimpanzee is violent, aggressive, and patriarchal. He takes females at will, sometimes killing his own kind, including infants. His social organization is somewhat militaristic, centered around an alpha male, to whom the other males are subordinate. Females are, in general, subordinate to males. Females mate only in estrus, and display their fertility through a temporary coloring of the genitals.

The bonobo, though sharing 99.6% of the chimpanzee's DNA, is very different. She is far more egalitarian (though somewhat hierarchical) in social organization, not particularly aggressive, and highly sexual (even using sex to resolve conflicts). She lives in a society that is as matriarchal as it is patriarchal, and can mate any time she pleases, choosing her partners rather than being chosen.

Ryan and Jethá argue that anthropologists who liken *Homo sapiens* to the chimpanzee miss the mark; we are far more similar to the bonobo, and thus our early social organization would more reasonably resemble theirs to that of the chimpanzee.

Human females, not males, drove human evolution.[18] A number of critical sexual features have made us who we are. We list them incidentally, with little thought of how each affects the other. But when we put them all together, we see that human females were no docile spoils of ape combat or docile sexual vessels – they were the driving force of our evolution.

Those features included:

- *The forward vulva.* Like the bonobo (and only the bonobo), the human female's vulva is forward, rather than oriented downward (see above). This led to…
- *Face-to-face mating.* Unlike the chimpanzee, who mates rearward (like horses and dogs), humans mate face-to-face; we are certainly capable of a wide range of mating positions – but face-to-face has unique characteristics that make a difference not only in sex, but in cognition, like…
- *Eye-gazing while mating.* Human beings, like bonobos, look into each other's eyes. This is a game-changer; it goes to the Theory of Mind, the concept of moving toward greater self-

---

[18] See *Lucy's Courtship: The Role of the Female in Human Sexual Evolution*, by the author.

awareness and understanding of others of our kind through the realization that they have inner lives similar to our own. This social cognition feature is present to at least a minimal degree in all primates, but is strongest in humans and bonobos – who also, as a result of face-to-face mating, practice...

- *Sexual kissing.*[19] Anyone who was ever a teenager knows that making out increases the likelihood of mating: the longer we engage in the almost inexplicable act of prolonged oral contact, which has no clear sexual value, the more we want to have sex. The reason is simple – during a "wet kiss," also called a French kiss, testosterone is transferred from the male to the female – which is absorbed directly into her bloodstream by the membranes of her mouth tissues, then converted into estradiol – which heightens her desire. Put simply, kissing increases the enjoyability, and thus the frequency, of sex – a reproductive advantage for the species. And this female facility for self-directed pleasure led to...

- *Hidden estrus.* Unlike all other primates (except the bonobo), the human female can mate at any time during her reproductive cycle, rather than only during fertility. She presents no outward sign of fertility to males. This increases her autonomy and potential selectivity in mate choice – and stands in opposition to the sexual aggression present among chimpanzee males, who compete violently because their choices of females are far more limited. And this female autonomy and selectivity in sexual choice gave human females an astonishing evolutionary power.

- *Mate selection by scent.* All else being equal, human females choose their partners based on how they smell. They do this instinctively, and they do it universally. Every woman living today has this innate tendency, whether she acts on it or not. And it gives her – and the human race overall – a huge advantage: when a woman chooses a partner based on scent, she is unconsciously choosing a partner based on the difference between her complex of genes that define the immune systems of her offspring, and that of the mate she has chosen – the greater the difference, the stronger the immune systems of the children of the mating. This ability

---

[19] Per *The Making of Star Trek*, by Gene Roddenberry and Stephen Whitfield (published in 1968), the network often sent down the memo, "Avoid the open-mouth kiss."

had to evolve, meaning females were the sexual choosers in prehistory. Men, notably, to not have this ability: they conform to the Captain Kirk method of selection – *two arms, two legs, two eyes, two boobs – we're good!*

The consequences of this chain are monumental.

To begin with, shared gaze deepened human consciousness – caused it to develop in ways it didn't in the chimpanzee. The chimpanzee does not follow the eye gaze of his peers – he follows their head and shoulder movements.

Humans (and the bonobo, who also shares eye-gaze during mating) follow the eye movements of other humans. Apart from strengthening mutual awareness, this ability enables others: we were able to communicate far more deeply, pre-language, than chimpanzees or other primates (apart from the bonobo). The survival benefit is obvious – deep communication, pre-language, enabled everything from tool-making to hunt-planning; and following eye movements, rather than head movements, helped us through the millennia we were prey to stronger, hungrier creatures: it enhanced the speed with which we could respond to the detection of predators.

The benefits of "sniffing" out a stronger match in mating had obvious benefits: with women unconsciously choosing partners who would yield offspring with stronger immune systems, we set the stage for our great diaspora – out-migration into regions of the world in which we did not evolve, where ecosystems differed – enhancing our diversity through adaptation to other climates and environments in which we might not otherwise have survived.

Finally, hidden estrus enabled gender equality, and made our limited sexual dimorphism practical: male and female could more practically work side-by-side when females shared, and were able to indulge by their own will, sexual desire and choice: rather than being objects of combat by needy males, they located sexual tension where it belonged – in the thrill of conjugation, rather than in disparity in supply and demand. Human males are, generally, calmer and more cooperative because human females are, ultimately, in charge of mating – whether that fact is acknowledged or not.

Division of labor only recently *became gender-based.* Adding to the mythology of the supremacy of human males in prehistory is the idea that gender-based division of labor has always been with us – that the men went out and hunted and the women stayed home and cooked, as has been the case for the past few thousand years.

"The rich archaeological record of the Middle Paleolithic[20] cultures in Eurasia suggests that earlier hominins pursued more narrowly focused economies, with women's activities more closely aligned with those of men with respect to schedule and ranging patterns than in recent forager systems," concluded Steven Kuhn, professor of anthropology at the University of Arizona[21]. Not until the Upper Paleolithic – less than 50,000 years ago – did broader economies emerge, with proliferation of roles and gender selection of labor, per Kuhn.

While Kuhn and his colleagues make the point that gender-based division of labor may have given *Homo sapiens* a strategic advantage over the Neandertals in Europe in the Upper Paleolithic, the fact is that the idea that human females have naturally done "women's work" isn't supported by the evidence. Women have worked alongside men, no matter the task at hand, for hundreds of thousands of years.

"There is still this wider perception that hunter-gatherers are more macho or male-dominated," said anthropologist Mark Dyble of University College London.[22] "We'd argue that it was only with the emergence of agriculture, when people could start to accumulate resources, that inequality emerged."

"Sexual equality is one of an important suite of changes to social organization, including things like pair bonding, our big social brains, and language, that distinguishes humans," he said. "It's an important one that hasn't really been highlighted before."

What's our conclusion from all of this? There's a reason Spock kneels next to Uhura as she makes emergency repairs to the ship's communication system and says, "I can think of no one better equipped to handle it, Ms. Uhura." Women can do any job men can do, and can often do it better. And that's not a case of "progress" – it's been true from the beginning, and remained true all along.

Reality: Females worked alongside males as equals, and their unique abilities and contributions were the drivers of human evolution...

---

[20] The period of history beginning roughly 300,000 years ago and ending roughly 50,000 years ago.

[21] *Current Anthropology*, Dec. 2008, Vol. 47, Issue 6, pp. 953-981.

[22] "Sex equality can explain the unique social structure of hunter-gatherer bands," *Science*, May 2015, Vol 348, Issue 6236, pp. 796-798.

The Empath

Myth: Early humans communicated by grunting and gesturing.

 Deanna Troi stands with the landing party in a chamber on Farpoint Station, as an unknown force tortures the duplicitous Zorn, who cries out that he doesn't know why he is being tormented, or what the unknown force wants of him.

"Not true," Deanna reports. "He does know."

Conveying his impressions of the living energy cloud that has killed members of his crew and, in his Starfleet past, the crew and captain of a ship he once served aboard, Kirk tells Spock and McCoy, "Inform [Starfleet] that we are pursuing the creature...to the location of its attack on the USS Farragut eleven years ago."

Spock is confused: "I do not understand, Captain."

And Kirk makes a startling claim: "In Garrovick's quarters, I said the scent of the creature was somehow different. Something in my mind said, 'Home'..."

Stranded on an unnamed planetoid with the long-missing Zefram Cochrane, Kirk, Spock and McCoy learn that a being of energy, with whom Cochrane has long acquaintance, has brought their shuttlecraft to this place – and that Cochrane can communicate with the creature, by letting it surround him.

"It's on a non-verbal level," he explains, "but I can usually get my message across."

These are just a few of many examples of non-verbal communication permeating the Trek canon. Other episodes – "The Empath," "Loud as a Whisper" – explore other variations. Bottom line: human beings can communicate in many ways, not just through language; and the science fiction machinations of telepathy are not required.

The fact that the human brain is able to find ways to interpret other human beings without the use of language is a more important chapter in the human story than you might think. The is persistent disagreement among anthropologists and evolutionary biologists as to when human being developed structured spoken language – estimates range from over 200,000 years ago to 60,000 years ago, with some maverick outliers at over 1 million years ago – but regardless of which of these is ultimately correct, the fact is that we know with reasonable certainty that we achieved astounding social order and solidarity well before spoken language entered the picture.

Pre-linguistic human beings were capable of magnificent cooperative feats. Before fully modern humans emerged (over 200,000 years ago), we were already tightly organized into efficient hunters, nimble migrants, effective planners.

How were these hunts planned? How were these migrations organized and led? How was the cornucopia of survival information required for this environmental dexterity communicated?

Looking into one another's eyes, as we've already noted, is a trait that separates human beings and our cousins, the bonobos, from all the rest. All the rest focus on head and shoulder movements and other cues for social communication.

Consider that we (and the bonobo) are, by far, the most social creatures on the earth, and have been for several million years. Consider also that we cannot attribute this great success, leveraging social communication for cooperation and survival, to language - for we have only had language for about 100,000 years, the most recent two percent of our ancestral line's existence.

How were we communicating before then, and how could we have done it so well?[23]

Before anyone shouts, "Telepathy!", let's hear from Donna Armstrong, a professor of epidemiology, commenting on the pre-linguistic origins of human cooperation:

> "Over a period of at least five million years, since the emergence of the hominid line, the capacity evolved for extremely sensitive emotional connecting with other group members. By signaling through fine-tuned muscles of the face and other body language, emotional approval and disapproval could be rapidly and very sensitively conveyed. Our first language - even of contemporary humans - is reading and responding to the unspoken emotional cues and signals of other people. We constantly practice an ancient, highly nuanced body language with each other. We especially read, in each other's faces, extremely rapid, subtle emotional signals, and these emotional experiences are a constant part of our cognitive processing of others and ourselves. Evolutionary selection for size and complexity of the brain system, along with upright stature and other adaptations, supported the development of his emotional experience and primary communication in humans."

It only takes a moment's thought to see that communication system still at work, doesn't it? And most of us have noticed that its absence in online digital communication often leads to misunderstanding and social chaos.

The take-home point: that we are gifted with the emotional richness of one another's faces makes human communication possible. It is not a gift

---

[23] This discussion of Donna Armstrong's observations on Paleolithic non-linguistic communication is taken from the essay collection *This Is What I'm Saying*, by the author.

to be taken for granted. Wise, perhaps, to set words aside, and simply listen by seeing.

And we've had this gift for hundreds of thousands of years.

The thing is – we don't use it anymore.

Reality: Human beings were almost unique among Earth's creatures in seeing themselves in others, able to understand one another intimately, long before actual language...

The Paradise Syndrome

Myth: Early humans were poverty-ridden and half-starving, barely scratching out an existence...

Part of our mythology about our most distant ancestors is that they were scavengers, constantly scrambling to survive in the face of horrific climate stresses, terrifying predators, and internal conflict.

Where do these ideas come from? They date back farther than Raymond Dart.

It was in fact Thomas Hobbes who introduced into Western civilization the concept of a brutish, scavenging forefather. Writing in the 17th century, the British philosopher built a case for the necessity of politics in human social order – and, in the process, defined the "natural" human, the creature inhabiting the Earth without benefit of modern sociopolitical organization:

> "In such condition," Hobbes wrote in his book *Leviathan*," there is no place for industry; because the fruit thereof is uncertain: and consequently no culture of the earth; no navigation, nor use of the commodities that may be imported by sea; no commodious building; no instruments of moving, and removing, such things as require much force; no knowledge of the face of the earth; no account of time; no arts; no letters; no society; and which is worst of all, continual fear, and danger of violent death; and the life of man, solitary, poor, nasty, brutish, and short."

Interesting as his ideas were, Hobbes was nonetheless far off base, writing without benefit of modern anthropology or even the core concepts of human prehistory brought forth by Charles Darwin two centuries later. He unwittingly set the tone for the early Enlightenment concept of prehistoric humanity – a portrait of a beast, unsophisticated and impoverished.

It turns out not to be the case.

We've already seen that early human beings were necessarily well-organized and socially self-aware. Modern anthropology's take on our Paleolithic knack for subsistence living is even more promising. Here's what neuroendocrinologist Robert Sapolsky, who studies primate social order, has to say:

> "People went and looked at [present-day hunter gatherers] closely (anthropologists in the Sixties) and discovered these people were not starving; these people were having a very comfortable existence in lots of ways. If you're going to be in the developing world, you would much rather be a hunter-gatherer than an agriculturalist or a nomadic pastoralist; you have a much better diet, far more variety, far more resistance to famine, because you're eating three hundred different plant species instead of the six or seven things you're cultivating; you have far less work – agriculturalists work like maniacs, these hunter-gatherers work three, four hours a day for their calories and spend the rest of their time doing social anthropology or whatever they do there; it's a much easier lifestyle."

In some ways, agriculture was truly a step forward: it enabled specialization, the luxury of dedicating some members of the tribe to functions only they could practice and fulfill. It enabled refined division of labor, beyond what was possible during our hunter-gatherer phase.

But it had its downside, enabling inequality, famine, disease, and other joyous steps forward. One thing it didn't do was empower us as survivors; we were that already. And it didn't lift us up from poverty – it sowed the seeds of poverty to come. We were doing just fine to being with.

Reality: Human beings were superb survivors, able to draw energy from the environment creatively and efficiently...

"A lot has changed in the past 300 years. People are no longer obsessed with the accumulation of things. We have eliminated hunger... want... the need for possessions. We've grown out of our infancy."

~Picard in 'The Neutral Zone'

That Which Survives

Myth: It was civilization that imbued humankind with common purpose.

Kirk and Kang stand together in the Enterprise *engine room, spurring their respective crewmembers to mocking laughter – ousting an alien intruder that has been feeding on their negative emotions.*

All of their animosities are set aside, as both sides unite to oppose their mutual enemy, which threatens them all with eternal torment, each at the hand of the other – joining in common purpose, as Kirk advocated to Bela Oxmyx and his rivals on Sigma Iotia, and to the warring leaders of Vendikar and Eminiar VII, and so many others...

A common theme in *Trek* is that a civilization is stronger when it is united in common purpose – an idea Kirk promoted in both the moment and, for civilizations he felt like meddling in, the long run.

Whether he was meddling or not, it's certainly true that nothing unites a society like common purpose. All too often, that purpose is war – but that very example underscores the point.

Anyone who has been to war, risked everything in defense of home, family and country, understands the concept of 'Band of Brothers' – a group of young men are thrown together by an imminent threat to their homeland, rapidly trained and shipped out to some front line where a formidable enemy waits, where bullets are flying and bombs exploding.

And those young men bond rapidly and deeply, to the point that the survivors will be reuniting a half-century later, to celebrate their bond and renew their mutual gratitude.

This experience is rare. Few things bring people together like the response to existential threat. In two world wars, we saw this response, this transformation that forever altered men in the battlefield, women supporting them in a wide range of roles, and the society they returned to serve.

Fighting to survive, side by side – it is hard to imagine a more powerful social force.

In the modern era, it is the rare exception: few of us fight for our lives, ever, let alone for extended periods, side by side with others. Our lives are very easy and trouble-free, compared to our distant ancestors – for whom the fight to survive, side by side, was never-ending, from birth to death.

A number of threats persisted for the 3+ million years the human line was evolving, but the greatest was predation: located in south-central Africa, we lived among the most vicious, efficient hunters roaming the Earth at that time – the members of the *Panthera* genus. The Big Cats.

We know from the ratio of skeletons recovered in Africa that Paleolithic humans had very limited lifespans. But this wasn't due to genetics – Cro-Magnon humans were genetically identical to us, and we can live more than 100 years. It wasn't due to famine – famine didn't exist; or disease, which existed, but which didn't impact us heavily until we began living in close, largely unsanitary groups.

We seldom lived to 30 because we were likely to be killed and eaten before we reached that age.

We noted previously (see "The Savage Curtain", page 24) that the predation of leopards, tigers, and other cats was systematic, and it took us many tens of thousands of years to develop defenses. During that phase of our physical and social evolution, our mutual reliance in detecting and fleeing predators, prior to (or upon) attack, necessarily required focused attention, strong communication, and an investment in one another's survival. The invention of the spear didn't diminish this reliance; if anything, it greatly strengthened it, because communication in coordinated counter-attack was necessarily even deeper, and the trust of the tribe in its defenders heightened, as they undertook risks previously unimagined, in defense of the group and their young.

And this wasn't the only mutual reliance: while the hunter-gatherer lifestyle offers a wide range of sustenance and many modes of acquiring food, it nonetheless requires deep mutual reliance and trust to cope with the migration of animals that could provide food, adapting to weather affecting the presence of edible plants, and anticipating cold weather and storms. Internally, cooperative efforts such as the manufacturing of survival-critical artifacts, maintenance of fire, and the preparation and distribution of food all required deep familial cooperation. The members of a human tribe were together 24/7 – sleeping, waking, hunting, mating, child-rearing – surviving. Birth to death, for hundreds of thousands of years.

Human beings are the ultimate cooperators.

It is difficult to imagine a more intimate life. It is hard to fathom deeper common purpose.

And if any further evidence of *Homo sapiens*' strong capacity for cooperation was the key to our eventual survival and dominance, our entry into Paleolithic Europe sets aside all doubt.

The Savanna Principle

Taking delight in the differences between human beings necessarily begins with enjoying them in the first place.

How this state is achieved and how it works, once achieved, are questions central to our understanding of human nature, and have been for thousands of years. Are human beings naturally competitive or cooperative? Are we instinctively wary of others, or inwardly welcoming? Are the answers to these questions the same today as they were 100,000 years ago, and if not, why not?

That human beings are the ultimate cooperators in the annals of life is beyond dispute: no other species comes close to having achieved what we achieve when we operate collectively, for good or ill. But what drives that cooperation? Economics? Improving our survival by controlling the environment? Tribal dynamics?

Satoshi Kanazawa[24], an evolutionary psychologist at the London School of Economics, had a different idea. In 2004, he proposed the Savanna Principle, which suggests that human beings remain adapted to the environment in which we evolved – central Africa – and that many of our modern-world dysfunction may be attributed to our inherent incompatibility with the environment we have created for ourselves. Our

---

[24] It should be noted that Kanazawa is a controversial figure in evolutionary psychology – not for his Savanna Principle, but for the contentious suggestion in other published work that disease and poverty are rampant in Africa because of lower native IQ, and the even more contentious suggestion that black women are objectively less attractive than other women. In response to these, his university forbade him from publishing in non-peer-reviewed sources for a period of one year, and 38 of his colleagues censured him in *American Psychology*.

ancient hunger for sugars, for instance – a survival advantage in an environment protein-rich and sugar-poor, where quick-hit energy and immediate storage of ingested carbohydrates could be a huge benefit – is extremely detrimental to our health in the modern era, where all foods are plentiful and none of us are ever tasked with fleeing from large, fast predators.

We are already neck-deep in that general idea, but Kanazawa adds a wrinkle that we can add to our thinking. The wrinkle we now add is the dopamine *ding*, that rewarding little boost we feel in our brains when we solve a problem, eat a tasty meal, or have sex. Dopamine is our inner assurance that all is right with the world – and we can tie it to a further thought of Kanazawa's.

That idea posits that human tribes on the savanna faced an almost endless series of challenges, puzzles and problems beyond the ken of any individual – and that a human tribe could, collectively, thrive in such a world far better than an individual. This idea, which he crafted with Norman Li of Singapore Management University, was dubbed the Savanna Theory of Happiness – that the impulse modern humans feel to be around other humans is a holdover from our savanna days, when there was pleasure in facing the dangers of the world surrounded by other problem-solvers.

(A corollary to this idea is its explanatory force regarding high-IQ individuals, who prefer solitude to a far greater degree – because, the theory suggests, they are superb problem solvers on their own, with less need for the emotional relief of a surrounding tribe.)

When we fold the dopamine *ding* into that theory, we take a huge leap forward: we have a physical, genetically-linked attribute of human cognition (dopamine receptivity) that supports the idea of group selection, that cooperative human groups are subject to an evolutionary driver above the level of personal survival and gene transmission.

We'll take this up in more depth later on.

Last Humans Standing:
Interspecies Cooperation

It wasn't just cooperation among ourselves that led humankind to survival and success - all primate species cooperate, living and thriving in social groups. *Homo sapiens*, however, took it to the next level: inter-species cooperation.

In 2009, Mietje Germonpre of the Royal Belgian Institute of Natural Sciences established a cranial distinction between canine species - a way of separating dogs from wolves. This development overturned previous estimates of the advent of the domestication of canines in human history (around 18,000 years ago), given the presence of much older skulls in Europe (32,000+ years).

This was a stunning finding. It basically established that when our species invaded and took Europe from the Neanderthals, we did so with canine assistance.

As strategic partnerships go, it couldn't have been a more perfect fit. Humans have an incredibly poor sense of smell, one of the worst in the animal kingdom; dogs, of course, rank near the top, giving Team Sapiens an overwhelming advantage in the hunt. Add to that their auditory range, which extends beyond that of humans, adding significantly to their value as trackers.

Moreover, dogs are possessed of almost human-like loyalty, strengthening the alliance beyond any other domestic bond between human and animal, before or since. Neanderthals couldn't possibly compete – and the question of how Cro-Magnon took over is answered: the human-canine partnership combined the traits of the world's most sensitive trackers with those of the world's most cooperative predators.

It was a piece that had been missing for some time. The fossil and climate records have already informed us of Neanderthal history: they were in Europe more than half a million years in advance of *Homo sapiens*. They had stronger, sturdier physiques; slightly larger brains; sophisticated group behaviors, even comparable culture. Cro-Magnon (modern) humans show up, and the Neanderthals are gone in an eye-blink (possibly as quickly as 2,000 years).

To some degree, we now know, we absorbed them: each of us carries at least a residual smudge of their DNA. But the fact is, we took their territory, and took it quickly. Per anthropologist Pat Shipman, it was human partnership with dogs that made the difference.

With his best friend at his side, the Cro-Magnon out-hunted the neighbors by a wide margin. Humans and dogs together were far more effective that humans alone - and remain so, as hunters, even today.

The Prehistory of Altruism

The German physicist Stefan Klein offers a bold new insight to our consideration of cooperation, and it's this: the purest form of cooperation is contributing with no thought of return – altruism. And in his view, it is altruism that ultimately defines us as human.

Reciprocity is doing something for someone, expecting them to do something in return; cooperation is working together in pursuit of a shared goal, expecting to benefit equally from the outcome. But altruism abandons these expectations; it is action taken on behalf of another person or the group for the sake of the action itself.

No other creature behaves in such a way.

Klein continues, building the case that altruism is innate – built into human genes, alongside cooperation and empathy. His case is simple: it is empirically demonstrable that acts of altruism evoke the same neurological satisfactions in human beings as sex or eating a tasty meal. When we perform an act of kindness or service to another person with no thought or expectation of reward, we feel a sense of pleasure and satisfaction – a *dopamine response*. No one teaches us this feeling; small children experience it when they share a cookie or a toy with a peer (in studies conducted to measure this, facial expressions and vocalizations were used as satisfaction measures).

We experience this pleasure even when the act is remote – when we don't see the response of the person to whom the kindness or service is offered. Anonymous altruism is, in fact, as pleasurable as an in-person act.

Empathy plays a role here. When we perform an altruistic act for another, we are acting in the confidence that their emotional response will be akin to what ours would be, were we on the receiving end of such an act.

And empathy, Klein points out, is a component of trust.

Acts of altruism, then, are signposts of empathetic bonding – and a trust-building mechanism. As such, altruism is elevated to a key influence in human social success.

The Origin of Trust

In *The Moral Molecule: The New Science of What Makes Us Good and Evil*, Paul Zak painstakingly explains how empathy arises in human beings, becoming trust, enabling our moral selves and social organization – by way of oxytocin.

Oxytocin is central to our neurological machinery, a key player in our emotional selves. It is a peptide hormone, playing roles in sex, birth, breastfeeding, and social bonding. It is the big moving part in the chain of experiences that makes us the most socially successful creatures on earth.

Oxytocin is the source of the contractions women experience in childbirth, a response to the stretching of the cervix; it subsequently enables lactation, triggering the letdown of milk, and its production is perpetuated by the stimulation of the nipples by a suckling infant.

That seems simple enough, but Zak elaborates in great detail. This birth/breastfeeding mechanism is only the beginning, however. A key point is that oxytocin isn't a female hormone; it is present in both genders, and has many functions beyond breastfeeding.

When an infant feels the skin of her mother's breast against her cheek, she will instinctively turn to the nipple. This 'latch' reflex facilitates mother-child bonding; the mother experiences warm, affectionate feelings for her child as a direct response to the flood of oxytocin.

The thing is... neither the release of oxytocin nor the feelings it inspires are limited to breasts and baby cheeks.

Gentle skin-to-skin contact *in general* inspires the release of oxytocin and its bounty of positive feelings. When we touch someone's face, embrace them, shake their hand, place an arm around them, we trigger a surge of oxytocin in them and in ourselves.

This, Zak explains, is where empathy ultimately arises. It signals to those we are close to that we are a source of warmth and comfort – and this leads to trust, which in turn leads to social cohesion within groups. Oxytocin intensifies in-group bonding.

That sounds like a pretty big leap. But it's been empirically tested.

One study[25] demonstrated that participants who received nasal infusions of oxytocin had stronger emotional responses to pictures of pained faces of in-group members than they did to pained expressions in out-group members. Further, oxytocin stimulates a desire to protect vulnerable in-group members in conflicts between groups: participants in another study[26] who received nasal oxytocin infusions presented more defensive behaviors toward in-group members than out-group members. Many variations on this theme have emerged in research: affection for one's nation, for instance, measured by feelings inspired when seeing the national flag, measurably increases when oxytocin is boosted.

And the neurological machinery that makes this deep bonding happen has been with us for hundreds of thousands of years; civilization has nothing to do with it.

Zak leaves us with a very broad statement about the crucial role of oxytocin:

> "The 'thou shalt' religious devotion that my mother tried
> to pound into me faded away a long time ago, but
> ironically, something at the core has remained. Oxytocin
> – a reproductive hormone – makes us moral, so

---

[25] "Oxytocin modulates the racial bias in neural responses to others' suffering", F. Sheng et al. *Biological Psychology* 92(2), 380-6.

[26] "Oxytocin motivates non-cooperation in intergroup conflict to protect vulnerable in-group members", C.K. De Drew et al, *PLOS ONE* 7(11).

ultimately, you could say that we are moral because of our origins as sexual creatures. Which harks back to that very Christian-sounding idea that God is love, or maybe that love is God. But as we saw, *eros* – sex – is only one kind of love, and oxytocin covers all the bases. Oxytocin makes us feel the love for others that's known as *philia*, the familial love known as *storge*, as well as *agape* – transcendence, which can be released during dance, meditation, and magic."

To me, God references notwithstanding, that's pretty *Trek*-sounding.

Reality: Common purpose evolved as a consequence of human capacity for deep cooperation, altruism, trust in one another and investment in one another...

The Needs of the Many

"Logic clearly dictates," Spock tells Kirk, "that the needs of the many outweigh the needs of the few."

"Or the one," Kirk says.

Homo sapiens is by far the most social species in existence, and outlived its sibling species through unprecedented cooperation – by meeting the needs of the many. What was the basis of this success? It was written in our genes...

Now that humankind has developed technology that allows us to observe the human brain while it's operating, we're beginning to make rapid progress in understanding how the mind works. And one finding in particular shines light on both our misunderstanding of the past and our problems in the present: we *literally* think differently from one another.

Recent studies in the neurological foundations of sociopolitical bias have set us on a path of discovery of brain differences that result in variations in both predispositions and behaviors, across a wide spectrum of cognitive features: creativity, risk aversion, empathy, response to authority, and a number of others. Put another way, there's more nature than nurture in our social thoughts, feelings and behaviors: our paths are not set in stone, but neither are we born *tabula rosa* – there is great diversity to be found in the brains of any nursery full of newborns.

Of course, there is plenty of nurture in the mix as we grow. The predispositions we're born with shape our responses to our social group as we learn to be part of it, but the social group itself provides the knowledge we need in order to express ourselves and interact with others. But more often than not, we are born into social groups that reinforce those predispositions nature has provided (more on this later) –

nature and nurture are often singing the same song, when it comes to the shaping of our behavior.

Cognitive Diversity

Several areas of the human brain play important roles in our social predispositions, and it's the study of these areas and how they vary that are opening up our understanding of cognitive diversity in human beings. Each of these areas can contain a range of tissue volume, and we are able to correlate that volume to ranges of social thought and behavior.[27] The result is that there are several prominent combinations of variation in these areas which produce predictable social orientations and worldview. Put another way, there are several cognitive "types" of human beings, genetically determined, each with social predispositions that serve particular functions in a human group.

The anterior cingulate cortex. The ACC is part of the corpus callosum, the tissue which integrates the two hemispheres of the brain. Among other things, the ACC is a hub for the processing of social interactions, empathy in particular; it facilitates error detection, monitors outcomes, and plays a role in action planning.

As such, the ACC is deeply involved in much if not most of our social behavior, playing a central role in evaluating our interactions and sending us signals when something is amiss.

The insula. The insula (insular cortex) is a kind of line judge for social emotion, calling out boundary violations. It regulates emotional response to disgust, which turns out to be strongly correlated to our core moral choices.[28] These responses in turn feed into our evaluation of social behaviors in others, empathy, and processing of social emotions.

The amygdala. Part of one of the most ancient assemblies in the brain (the limbic system), the amygdala is actually a pair of components - one port, one starboard.

---

[27] "Political Orientations Are Correlated with Brain Structure in Young Adults," *Current Biology*, Vol. 21, Issue 8, pp. 677-680, April 2011.

[28] "Disgust as embodied moral judgment," Jonathan Haidt, et al, *Personality & Social Psychology Bulletin* 34, 1096-109.

The starboard amygdala is where fear is processed, and where emotional responses to episodic memories occur, tying past events back to our feelings about those events.

Dopamine receptivity. Dopamine is the neurotransmitter that 'rewards' the brain when good things happen. Not surprisingly, it kicks in as part of the cognitive equation in everything from creativity to sex to social media response. Dopamine produces a high, from which other brain processes then emerge.

Low receptivity to dopamine is the basis of ADD, the quest of the brain's attentional mechanisms to scan for novelty in the environment, with all the emotional peripherals that implies. High receptivity to dopamine can result in anxiety, as the brain is rapidly satisfied with the stimulus at hand and desires no more – which also carries some emotional consequences.

There are others, but these are the big ones. Variation in these brain areas gives humankind a cognitive diversity that allows groups of human beings to solve more problems – and solve them more effectively – than any one human being could alone.

And since this variety is genetically transmitted, it's been a feature of human social existence for a very long time.

Chuck and Roger in the Middle Paleolithic

Chuck is a young Cro-Magnon in the Middle Paleolithic, part of a tribe that hunts and gathers in South-Central Africa. Possessing a large ACC, a large insula, and a small amygdala – as well as having low dopamine receptivity - he is a skilled tracker, leading one of his tribe's hunting teams. He is inventive, adept at detecting patterns. He has found that his team performs best when they pool their insights and knowledge of environment, weather, and sign. He performs best, knowing that the portion of the tribe back at camp is safe; as a consequence, he could be called a risk-taker.

Roger is a member of Chuck's tribe. His cognitive features are the opposite of Chuck's – smaller ACC and insula, larger amygdala, high dopamine receptivity. He has little aptitude for pattern detection but possessed of uncommon diligence and alertness. He works third shift, keeping the basecamp's fire going at night, which provides warmth within and protection from the predators without. He is uninterested in pooled insights or deliberation - he is a man of action. He is more afraid of the dangers around the tribe than most others, but this makes him the ideal security officer.

Chuck tends to take his time making a decision. When tracking a migrating herd, he and his team pick up on many signs and choose their course carefully. They are not impulsive, but deliberate. Roger and those like him, on the other hand, are very impulsive, very reactive; they have to be, because a single snapping of a twig in the shadows over their shoulders might signal the approach of a predator. That's not a moment for lengthy contemplation.

Chuck seeks consensus; Roger issues and obeys commands. Chuck scans for opportunities; Roger scans for threats. Chuck responds to novelty, Roger to a safe status quo.

Chuck and Roger represent opposite ends of the cognitive type spectrum – they are as different as can be – but each fills an essential role in tribal survival; it is difficult to imagine human survival in the Paleolithic without them. And between them are people of still more cognitive types, each with a different combination of strengths and skills, each contributing something meaningful and different.

This mix of diverse reasoning styles, differing decision-making impulses and viewpoints was a tremendous survival advantage across hundreds of thousands of years, as early humans navigated an Ice Age landscape packed with flesh-eating predators. The meeting of the tribe's needs, under such tense conditions, required more than just fast reflexes (though those were certainly important); it required
diversity not just in skills, but in thought. We could not have survived without that.

And that hasn't changed.

The Evolution of Cooperation

In his book *Why We Cooperate*, developmental psychologist Michael Tomasello addresses the following question: is cooperation between human beings a naturally emergent behavior or a learned one?

Either way, it's great that it exists, but the implications for our thesis – that human beings possess the inherent goodness in which Gene Roddenberry believed – are profound: if the former, then we have within us what we need to achieve a fully humanist future; if the latter, then it will be a far greater struggle, getting where we want to be.

Tomasello begins by pointing to research[29] demonstrating that infants as young as 18 months overwhelmingly attempt to assist adults whose hands are full. He cites this as one of five reasons to believe that this cooperative impulse in very small children is a naturally emergent human trait. It's the first of five:

1. Very small children impulsively help others without prompting or training;
2. Parental reward does not alter the outcome of #1; the child will impulsively help with or without reward;
3. Chimpanzee infants exhibit the same behaviors;
4. Human children exhibit the behavior across a diverse range of cultures;
5. Experiments have shown that helping behavior in young children is mediated by empathy – they will tend to help an adult they perceive to be a victim before helping another.

Tomasello continues to methodically develop a portrait of cooperation as evolutionary, building toward this conclusion: "...the changes we see in human societies beginning with the advent of agriculture and cities are not due, on anyone's account, to any kind of biological adaptation," he wrote. "The changes would seem to be sociological only, given their recency and the fact that by this time modern humans were already spread out all over the glove (so that a species-wide biological change was highly unlikely). What this means is that most, if not all, of the highly complex forms of cooperation in modern industrial societies – from the United Nations to credit card purchases over the Internet – are built primarily on cooperative skills ant motivations biologically evolved for small-group interactions: the kinds of altruistic and collaborative activities that we have seen here in our simple studies of great apes and young children."

We have good reason to believe, then, that the deep cooperation that binds not just humanity but all the worlds of the Federation in Roddenberry's 23rd century doesn't need to be contrived; it just needs to be awakened.

---

[29] *Not by Genes Alone: How Culture Transformed Human Evolution*, Peter Richardson and Robert Boyd. University of Chicago Press, 2006.

Lost in Space

Genetic variety in both our ancient (limbic) and modern (cortical) brain components – those contributing to social reasoning, in particular – gives us a group of distinct cognitive "types," each with different cognitive strengths and decision-making style. No one human mind can encompass the variety expressed by this range of distinct types; it takes a group of humans – a diverse group, with many persons of each type – fully express the potential of human reason and decision-making. And that potential, by evolution's hand, is how humankind has managed to meet the needs of the many, since our beginnings.

Cooperation among humans possessing these diverse cognitive types

The problem is… we've lost our way. Our modern social organization robs of us the value of the cognitive diversity that we absolutely will need to meet the challenges that threaten us, both today and tomorrow.

How we lost our way, and what we can do about it, will be taken up in the pages to follow.

The High Ground

Myth: Human morality is a product of reason, a consequence of civilization.

"Morality dictates that we help." ~Emergency Medical Hologram, "Warhead", Star Trek: Voyager

Through the lens of 20th century sociology, human beings are seen as inherently selfish – guided by self-interest, not group-interest. The patriarchal religions, of course, reinforce this idea, preaching that children are born "evil", and must have that evil replaced with divine purpose.

It is, in fact, the moral frames that human society implements which settle the question: our moral systems demonstrate our affinity for the group, our respect for others, and our valuation of those things we hold in common.

Until very recently in history, religion postured as the sole source of human morality. Even today, many religious people cling to the claim that without God, humans cannot manage to behave in morally sound ways. Human morality emanates from a divine source, they claim, and without that divinity, we are nothing more than depraved animals.

The Enlightenment did much to dispel such notions (though the Greeks, and Socrates in particular, were way out front). Moral behavior and moral decision-making came to be seen as coming from within humankind, rather than from above; but even so, this human-sourced morality was framed as a rational process – a product of reason that arrived with the dawn of civilization. But that turns out not to be the case.

How Morality Evolved

We've arrived at a critical fork in the road: if we are inherently self-oriented, rather than group-oriented, then our morality can be seen as a created thing, an innovation designed to curb our selfishness and allow us to live together without killing each other; if, on the other hand, we are inherently group-oriented, then our morality is likewise innate, something that has been with us all along, not a product of reason or civilization.

Put another way, we have a crucial question to answer: was morality invented, or did it evolve?

If it evolved, then it supports our thesis that humankind has had that Roddenberry spark for hundreds of millennia.

In his book *A Natural History of Human Morality*, Michael Tomasello compares the various theories of the evolution of morality, then produces one of his own. In doing so, he addresses a long-standing problem in the study of moral evolution: some researchers have looked into it in the context of small human tribes; others have sought to understand it in the broader context of the early city-states. Tomasello's own work sought to produce a theory that encompassed both.

In doing so, he notes that "early humans evolved a new moral psychology for face-to-face dyadic engagement in collaborative contexts. There is much evidence that dyadic interactions have unique qualities involving such things as eye contact, voice direction, and postural adjustments during communication, such that some anthropologists have posited a human 'interaction engine', geared for face-to-face dyadic interactions, as the explanation for virtually all forms of uniquely human sociality.

"Moreover, a number of the most basic forms of human social interaction are fundamentally dyadic, for example, friendship, romantic love, and conversation," he continued, "and the evolved emotions associated with these dyadic relationships are qualitatively distinct from anything associated with group interactions."

In other words, human moral psychology began not for the betterment of human groups, but the betterment of individual relationships – *second-person engagement*.

As for the emergence of large groups, Tomasello specifies a necessary consequence of second-person engagement – *group-minded morality*, wherein personal moral behaviors evolved into cultural group markers, reflecting the group's time-and-place context.

Taking into account the work done previously on the problem, he notes that there are three paradigms: evolutionary ethics; moral psychology; and gene-culture co-evolution.

Evolutionary ethics

Tomasello reviews the concept of evolutionary ethics, which focuses on *reciprocity* as the core of moral evolution: if humans behave such that a benevolent act inspires one in return, then the group has a greater chance of survival. He cites Richard Alexander's *The Biology of Moral Systems* as a showcase of this idea, adding that primatologist Frans de Waal embellished it with the critical importance of empathy (in both humans and lower primates).

He further cites Elliott Sober and David Sloan Wilson, whose 1998 work *Unto Others: The Evolution and Psychology of Unselfish Behavior* suggests that persistent patterns of sympathetic behavior and mutual helpfulness initiated a group selection process, empowering human groups that presented those patterns.

He also cites Christopher Boehm[30], who suggested that as early humans transitions from ape-like dominance-based organization to more egalitarian models, the importance of *selection by reputation* was established: if an individual behaved in a consistently moral manner, practicing reciprocity and empathy and helpfulness, then these things would become known about him, even to those who did not know him well. Moreover, Boehm suggested that coalitions would form to both reward moral behavior and punish transgression (cheating, bullying), making reputation a key personal concern, reinforcing the overall moral frame of the group. Finally, wrote Tomasello, Boehm had added that the internalization of selection by reputation had led to the development of *moral conscience* – the sense of guilt humans experience when they know they've transgressed against others in some way, even if their transgression has gone undetected.

And then there's Nicolas Baumard, J.B. Andre and Dan Sperber,[31] who underscored that selection by reputation resulted in *moral authenticity*: "The most cost-effective way of securing a good moral reputation may well consist in being a genuinely moral person."

Moral psychology

Evolutionary ethics offers some really good stuff, per Tomasello, but it is ultimately insufficient: there was too much it didn't adequately account

---

[30] See *Hierarchy in the Forest: The Evolution of Egalitarian Behavior*, Harvard University Press, 1999.

[31] "A Mutualistic approach to morality", *Behavioral and Brain Sciences* 36(1), 59-122, 2013.

for – aspects of moral psychology including joint commitments and promises, the creation and enforcement of social norms, and self-regulation of responsibility, obligation and guilt.

"Our view is thus that the main limitation of these various accounts in evolutionary ethics is that they do not appreciate sufficiently the way that human morality depends on the sense of "we" and self-other equivalence as individuals interact socially with cooperative motives and attitudes on the proximate psychological level."

Tomasello writes that *interdependence* is more powerful than the combination of reciprocity and sympathy in defining human moral behavior. This speaks to more specific biological features of humans with evolutionary impact given moral behaviors, specifically the neurophysiology of intuitive impulses, especially in the domain of harm.

There is a near-universal set of such intuitions, he points out, referencing the famous Trolley Problem[32] and the fact that responses to the problem are generally the same the world over, across cultures. Human beings, in general, have the same emotional responses to thoughts of harm to self or others. Tomasello references the work of John Mikhail[33], which suggests that a key feature of these universal responses is "judgment of blame when someone intentionally harms someone else, but absolution when the intentional act that causes harm was aimed at something good (and there were no viable alternatives available)."

We've lifted moral behavior and decision-making out of the realm of reason, then, and into the realm of emotion and intuition. Tomasello at this point defers to psychologist Jonathan Haidt, the pacesetter in moral psychology, who has stated plainly his belief that explicit reasoning about moral issues amounts to rationalization, which "justifies the already-made intuitive judgment. Its function is to persuade others that this judgment is the best one and so they should support it in any kind of dispute." Actual

---

[32] The Trolley Problem is one of the most famous and popular thought experiments. Suppose you are standing near a trolley track. There is a runaway trolley, heading for five workmen ahead on the track. You happen to be standing next to a switch that can shift the trolley to another track – but there is a hobo asleep on the track, who will be killed. You can save five by killing one. *What do you do?* Now comes the Fat Man Option: same problem, but instead of standing near the track switch, you are on a bridge above. There is a fat man next to you. By pushing him off the bridge onto the track, you can stop the trolley before it hits the five men – but he will die? *What do you do?* Almost universally, those presented with these problems report that they would take the first action – pulling the switch – but would not take the second, pushing the fat man off the bridge, despite the fact that the outcomes are identical.

[33] "Universal moral grammar: Theory, evidence and the future". *Trends in Cognitive Science*, 11(4), 143-142.

moral decisions are "innate predispositions that lead to quick, intuitive moral judgments, often laden with emotion."

Haidt's work includes the proposal that human moral judgments, emotionally impulsive in their nature, rely on five "pillars" - authority vs. subversion; care vs. harm; loyalty vs. betrayal; fairness vs. cheating; and purity vs. disgust. Tomasello notes that Haidt's research has demonstrated that the diversity in moral judgments that present in any population can be accounted for by where individuals sit on the spectrum of each pillar.

Haidt's model plugs into evolution as group selection, with each individual's moral adaptation tied to the quality of the group-minded moral frame at work; the higher the level of moral thought and behavior of individuals, the more successful the group, setting up a feedback loop that improves group-mindedness over time.

Gene-culture co-evolution

If moral impulses are emotional and intuitive in nature, and if the moral judgments of individuals set up and perpetuate group-minded moral norms and expectations, then human cultures must be accounted for, according to Tomasello. What is the role of culture in shaping those moral norms and expectations? They clearly differ significantly across cultures, both today and throughout recorded history. It is safe to assume the same was true in prehistory.

Tomasello then cites Joan Miller[34], who has proposed that individuals tend not to think of themselves as morally autonomous, but "as operating in subordination to natural law and objective obligation as set forth in the various practices and doctrines of their culture."

He proposes that theoretical human group selection manifests in the real world as cultural group selection, that "once cultures began evolving, different cultural groups could compete with one another, such that those with the most cooperative individuals would very likely do best. There were thus selection pressures within each cultural group for imitation and conformity, especially of successful individuals... humans thus have evolved, in a process of gene-culture co-evolution, both cooperative tendencies and 'tribal instincts' for living and functioning effectively in cultural groups."

Even so, Tomasello notes that this co-evolution can only explain recent human evolution, as human beings have only been creating cultures of the sort described above for the past 10,000 years or so; it cannot account for the origins of social institutions themselves: "These species-universal skills

---

[34] "Cultural diversity in the morality of caring: Individually oriented versus duty-based interpersonal moral codes", *Cross Cultural Research*, 28(1), 3-39.

and motivations would have needed to be in place before such processes of cultural evolution could have gotten started... cultural group selection is thus clearly an important part of the overall story, but only, we would claim, at the very end."

Even though the origins of human morality are not yet fully accounted for in the ideas articulated above, Tomasello has answered our original question: did we invent moral reasoning in the context of civilization, or is it built into us?

The nomenclature of contemporary psychology includes *Type I* and *Type II* references to cognitive processes: Type I cognition is intuitive and immediate, and often emotional; Type II cognition is the opposite – explicit reasoning achieved over time. Tomasello's account clearly places moral behavior and decision-making within Type I.

Put another way, moral impulses reside deeper in the human brain than our centers of reasoning; they are emotional, rather than intellectual, in nature. We have carried them within us, not for thousands of years, but for hundreds of thousands.

Tomasello's focus on interdependence takes us beyond that original question, however; it provides a framework for understanding how the *concept* of morality evolved.

Having pointed out the inadequacies of reciprocity as an explanation of human moral psychology, Tomasello's exploration of interdependence as an extension of moral psychology that is in harmony with Mikhail and Haidt and Miller, as well as the idea of gene-culture co-evolution, provides an account of how it fills in the blank the latter leaves unanswered: granting that morality evolved, rather than an artifact of reason, how did it precede human culture?

If paleolithic humans were not just mutually dependent, but perpetually *conscious* of that interdependence, Tomasello argues, then reciprocity and empathy and helpfulness begin to transcend mere barter, becoming genuine caring about others and their well-being; giving to others and helping them as a matter of course makes social life less transactional, and more about mutual investment in a shared future.

Moreover, he continues, interdependence is the core of shared intentionality – mutual goals and common behavioral patterns, which led to the evolution of new cognitive skills, such as cooperative communication, leading in turn to *thinking* morally, applying cognitive structure to facilitate both second-person engagement dyadics and group-minded norms. Put another way, Tomasello demonstrates that interdependence as a theoretical component of moral psychology explains how we came to be conscious of morality, hundreds of centuries before the invention of culture.

Reality: Human morality is innate, and has resided within us since long before the dawn of civilization.

"All of man's troubles have arisen from the fact that we do not know what we are and do not agree on what we want to be."

~Jean Bruller

The Cloud Minders

The Temple at Göbekli Tepe

And, finally - a mystery.

In 1995, a German archaeologist named Klaus Schmidt followed up on a site in Southern Turkey. Previously charted but unexplored by a team from the University of Chicago in the 1960s, the site was an unknown - but Schmidt was feeling antsy, and was up for a long dig.

He and his team spent the next 20 years unearthing the largest Neolithic structures in history - 200 T-shaped stone pillars, megaliths, arranged in 20 circles. The site is so large that only 5 percent of it has been excavated, to date (those ground-penetrating radar has mapped most of the rest).

Twenty times the size of Stonehenge, Göbekli Tepe covers an area the size of 12 football fields. Its pillars are six meters high and weigh up to 20 tons each. There is no structure like it anywhere in the world.

Here's where things get weird. Göbekli Tepe was built 11,500 years ago - *pre-dating human civilization*- by hunter-gatherers (we know this from the artifacts surrounding the site).

In other words, this astonishing accomplishment of human engineering basically occurred before anything like human engineering was thought to exist. The tooling and methods needed to cut and transport stones of such immense size were not thought to exist until 5,000 years later. Moreover, its construction would have required far more than a single tribe of hunter-gatherers - many hundreds of people would have had to work on building the site for many decades. No such social organization was thought to exist at that time; nor would it, it has previously been thought, for thousands of years.

Thought by some to be a temple of some kind (at a point in history when the idea of 'buildings' had not yet taken hold), Göbekli Tepe, like

Stonehenge and other similar monuments, is an astronomical calculator; allowing for the passage of more than 10,000 years, its adjusted orientation charts the rising point of the sun in relation to the solstices and equinoxes - thousands of years before humans were thought to have had any understanding of astronomy.

How is such a thing even possible?

How did *Homo sapiens*, still just a few centuries out of the last ice age, muster such a staggering vision? What would motivate early humans to build such a structure, to invest decades and millions of man-hours in its construction?

Where did the knowledge to build like that come from? How did we come to understand the motions of the sun and stars so early? What motivated the establishment of the social organization necessary to pull it off?

The answer has to be that we had already achieved that knowledge, that understanding, that motivation. Put simply, we in the present have severely underestimated our distant grandparents.

We may never know the exact progression of events and milestones that led to Göbekli Tepe. So many pieces are missing, and the window of time in which to search is so small.

If nothing else, however, Göbekli Tepe stands as a reminder of just how inadequate our portrait of early humanity really is. Whatever the details, the general reality is that we were not brutish, warlike thugs, duking it out on the savanna, fighting over females and gazelle carcasses: we were certainly, somehow, cooperative and industrious beings of strong kinship, able to work together in common purpose for indefinite periods, capable of looking far ahead.

"No, ancient astronauts did not build the pyramids—human beings built them, because they're clever and they work hard. And Star Trek *is about those things."*

~Gene Roddenberry

The naked now

Heading into the present, we now know more than we did – *much* more – than we knew in 1966, when *Star Trek* debuted. Our picture of humankind's infancy, though still incomplete, is much more encouraging today than it was then.

To summarize:

- We were not violent, brutish 'killer apes' - on the contrary, we were prey, bound together in survival-critical cooperation, exploring life and facing death together as no species before had ever done;
- We were not loosely associated nomads, wandering aimlessly - we were well-organized, systematically efficient clans with distributed leadership and a deep knowledge of our environment, able to eat well and protect ourselves in a wide range of terrains;
- We were not grunting savages, coercing one another with aggression - we were sophisticated, empathic communicators, highly sensitive to one another's emotions and our mutual humanity, long before the advent of language;
- Human females were not sex toys, battle trophies, or beasts of burden - they were social and intellectual equals, sharing in leadership and innovation;
- We were not poverty-ridden wraiths, barely able to feed ourselves – we were knowledgeable and efficient in self-sustenance, generating more than enough to feed the clan in only a few hours a day;
- We were not selfish, autonomous beings struggling to work together – we were increasingly altruistic with every evolutionary step, each contributing for the

common good as a matter of course... master cooperators, even across species boundaries;
- We were, somehow, capable of amazing intellectual leaps, engineering wonders and complex social cooperation, even before we mastered the practice of permanent settlement.
- We were, put simply, fully developed humanists – working together cooperatively, building together industriously, exploring together adventurously, sharing with each other unselfishly, and loving each other intimately.

So what went wrong?

"The future is already here;
it's just unevenly distributed."

~William Gibson

Mirror, Mirror:

The Distorted Human Present

"I believe that the extraterrestrials created by the confabulations of science fiction serve us in an important way: they improve reflection on our own condition."

~Edward O. Wilson

The Enemy Within

A change in course, and the unleashing of an inner beast...

An ion storm, a tense beam-up – and Kirk, McCoy, Scotty and Uhura find themselves in an uncomfortable alternate reality, surrounded by very dark, very different versions of the shipmates they know. This reality is shaped more or less like their own, but the humanist virtue pervading the universe living in their memories is gone, replaced by a colder, more authoritarian doppelgänger – a place inhabited by humans are decidedly less than they have the potential to be...

Where did we go wrong?

If *Homo sapiens* was doing so well for so long, how did we end up in the mess we're in today?

The answer is, one step at a time, and with a few very misguided steps in particular.

In the space of a few centuries, humankind swung from a Paleolithic zenith of cooperation, peaceful cohabitation and growing innovation and industry, to factionalization, patriarchy, and social dominance. Put another way, we ceased to mimic the culture of our bonobo cousins, and began to resemble more closely the chimpanzee.

"No matter what the hunter-gatherer character, however, it is important that we understand it, because in doing so we begin to define human nature. If there is an inherent nature in humans, it is a product of evolution. Evolutionary pressures take a long time to enter and to leave our genome. Our kind has spent at least 290,000 years as hunter-gatherers, only 10,000 as agricultural people, making the latter way of living a relatively brief and novel experiment. Only small traces of agricultural life can be read in our genes. We still run on hunter-gatherer software."

~Richard Manning

The Devil in the Dark

Distortion: The advent of agriculture, animal domestication and permanent settlement made us civilized.

McCoy, under the influence of the spores, slugs colony leader Elias Sandoval across the jaw. As Sandoval drops, both begin to shake off the influence.

"Sorry, Sandoval," McCoy says. "I don't know what made me do that."

Sandoval's mind is elsewhere: "We've done nothing here," he says. "No accomplishments, no progress. Three years wasted. We wanted to make this planet a garden."

That impulse – the systematic growing and harvesting of food – has been the work of 300 generations of human beings. Its origins, around the end of the last ice age, mark the first definitive step toward what we think of as civilization. It enabled us to draw 50 times as much energy from the land around us, and to store that energy. This in turn made it possible for us to turn our efforts to tasks other than the gathering of food for survival – building places to live, constructing fences, developing new technologies to facilitate a new way of living.

But agriculture was, at best, a mixed blessing. Contemporary anthropologists are cautionary in their characterization of its impact on human development.

"Agriculture was one of the great stupid mistakes in human history," said Prof. Robert Sapolsky of Stanford University. "That was a bad move! The main advantage of agriculture is that is allows you to concentrate capital and resources in the hands of a few people and start making stratified societies and all sorts of nasty stuff…"

According to Israeli historian Yuval Noah Harari, "The Agricultural Revolution certainly enlarged the sum total of food at the disposal of humankind, but the extra food did not translate into a better diet or more leisure. Rather, it translated into population explosions and pampered elites. The average farmer worked harder than the average forager, and got a worse diet in return. The Agricultural Revolution was history's greatest fraud."

And this from American anthropologist Jared Diamond:

"Hunter-gatherers practiced the most successful and longest-lasting life style in human history. In contrast, we're still struggling with the mess into which agriculture has tumbled us, and it's unclear whether we can solve it. Suppose that an archaeologist who had visited from outer space were trying to explain human history to his fellow spacelings. He might illustrate the results of his digs by a 24-hour clock on which one hour represents 100,000 years of real past time. If the history of the human race began at midnight, then we would now be almost at the end of our first day. We lived as hunter-gatherers for nearly the whole of that day, from midnight through dawn, noon, and sunset. Finally, at 11:54 p. m. we adopted agriculture. As our second midnight approaches, will the plight of famine-stricken peasants gradually spread to engulf us all? Or will we somehow achieve those seductive blessings that we imagine behind agriculture's glittering facade, and that have so far eluded us?"

Agriculture was unquestionably a Pandora's box for humanity's development. We've listed the pros; here are the cons:

- *Property*. With permanent settlements came a commitment to stay in one place, and a need to protect the land from outside invasion, and internal struggle over who owned what piece. For the first time ever, human beings had true motivation to fight not just the environment and predation, but each other;
- *Inequality*. With property came the potential for some to have more than others;
- *Misogyny*. With systematic division of labor came the tendency to relegate less desirable tasks to those who were physically weaker;

- *Inheritance.* With ownership of land came the impulse to secure the land as an economic advantage for one's own offspring, bringing about the development of social classes;
- *Famine.* Humankind went from eating 300+ different things to three or four grains and five or six animals; as we lost the freedom to move from place to place, we became vulnerable to food shortage;
- *Disease.* It became possible, through food accumulation, to gather populations beyond Dunbar's Number in one place, bringing about the spread of disease – often occurring because of constant proximity to domesticated animals.

Not quite what we bargained for.

Agriculture was, in many ways, a step forward survival-wise, for the species as a whole; but it was a giant step backward in our social evolution, bringing with it a weaker and more vulnerable way of living in exchange for the added security of stored food.

But no longer did we stand and fall together, live and die together; now it truly was everyone for themselves…

How Agriculture begat Religion, changing everything

Before moving on, a few words about how religion became a thing.

Futurist Yuval Noah Harari has noted that the modern era, which has steadily increased the existential and spiritual self-sufficiency of humankind as religion has receded, faces the problem of infusing life with meaning in a post-religion world.

That challenge has been met, he writes, by humanism, which he defines as "a revolutionary new creed that conquered the world during the last few centuries...the humanist religion worships humanity, and expects humanity to play the part that God played in Christianity and Islam, and that the laws of nature played in Buddhism and Daoism."

"Whereas traditionally the great cosmic plan [of religion] gave meaning to the life of humans," he continues, "humanism reverses the roles and expects the experiences of humans to give meaning to the cosmos."

Humanism, he writes, creates meaning for a meaningless world; it calls upon us to draw the meaning of our own lives from our inner experiences, and then to extend that meaning to the universe as a whole. Humankind, in Harari's summary, is the author of meaning.

In his book *Homo Deus*, this idea is presented as the best path forward for humanity. But in reality, it is more; it's a return to the path we originally walked.

Religion has been with us for a little over 12,000 years, in the best guesses of modern anthropologists and evolutionary psychologists like Azim Shariff, who suggests that 'God' was invented when agriculture began at the end of the last Ice Age, and large communities became possible – communities where it was impossible to police the behaviors of all, making it necessary to invent an all-seeing, all-punishing policeman.

But humankind has been around far longer than 12,000 years. In our present form – *Homo sapiens* – we've walked the earth for almost 300,000 years, and in less advanced form, ten times that long.

Were those thousands of centuries meaningless?

The millions of humans who lived and died in those years had brains like ours, communicated by language as we do (at least for the past 100,000 years or so), and built lives of shared experience, just like us. To read Harari without keeping this in mind is to passively assume that those millions of lives had no meaning – that "meaning", in the sense that we use it today, only came about with the invention of religion.

But is that even plausible?

The creation of meaning is built into the human brain. It isn't an invention of philosophers or poets or pastors; it's a natural function of the conscious mind. We are, each of us, makers of meaning.

This is why the question of meaning in our lives and in the universe around us matters so much in the first place: meaning necessarily exists in the mind, as it is an idea; and we all hunger for it, which tells us it's both natural and a function of mind.

If we've had it all along, then what is meaning, and where did it go?

The first clue can be found in the assumption that God(s) was/were ever a source of meaning; if we created God, then by definition, we are not only seekers of meaning – we are the *creators* of meaning. Our need for it follows our production of it.

Then we must accept that of all the life on Earth – as far as we know – and, for that matter, in all of time and space – as far as we are able to know – we are the only beings like ourselves to ever emerge, to ever get this far. We are on the leading edge of meaning; we are, in the universe, its sole source, its only repository.

Finally, we consider that while we may search for meaning as individuals, while we may each come up with solitary solutions in that quest, meaning itself is a community trait; when we find it, we share it, and it becomes a tying bind. Whatever distortions religion introduced into the nature and application of meaning, it positively underscores that meaning, by definition, is a group force. We create it together; we perceive it together; we enjoy it together. It nurtures us as one.

In our final analysis - *we* are meaning. We, humanity, *are meaning*.

We *define* meaning. And if we've lost our innate sense of that, it's because our attention has been long diverted, obfuscated by emotional plunder and garish charlatanry.

We are not, then, robbing the gods. We are not overweening usurpers or pretenders in taking up Harari's call; we have always been his cosmic adjudicators, the chancellors of ultimate truth. Why? Because no others in creation can take up the task. It has always been ours. And we are, in the end, our own answer: humanity isn't taking meaning over; we're taking meaning back.

"Human nature is the ensemble of hereditary regularities in mental development that bias cultural evolution in one direction as opposed to others and thus connect genes to culture in the brain of every person."

~Edward O. Wilson

The Will of Landru

Distortion: It is natural and good to congregate with the like-minded.

Harry Mudd has found paradise. His appropriated spacecraft, having suffered damage, has led him to a planet off the beaten path, populated only by androids – several hundred thousand of them, divided into a number of sub-groups, and every member of every sub-group identical in appearance and behavior...

...and all of them subordinate to a single leader who thinks and decides for them.

It looks very much like a satirical representation of life on Earth, as it has been for most of recorded history.

Call it *cognitive clustering*.

Once human beings started settling permanently in one place, growing wheat and raising animals to eat, it became possible for populations beyond the Dunbar Limit – more than 150 people – to live together in one place.

This was unprecedented in human history – we had never lived like this before. The migratory nature of human tribal existence made it impractical, and our brains couldn't deal with that many people anyway. Both the environment and our social brain tissue kept us below the 150-person limit.

But a village by a river – that's a different story. The nutritional yield per acre of farmed wheat is, at worst, about fifty
times that of wild plants. And animals you can kill and eat without having to track and hunt them? It was an irresistible deal for countless thousands of human tribes.

It led us into a dark tunnel from which we have yet to emerge.

When human beings live in close community, living their entire lives around the same small group of people, they are exposed to the different thoughts and minds and decision-making abilities of one another in roughly equal measure.

But when several hundred people live in close proximity, it becomes impossible to know everyone in the community intimately, because of our social cognition limitations – but it *is* possible for the community to split up into sub-groups, based on a new discriminatory criterion – like-mindedness.

Suddenly, human communities could segregate into clusters of people who thought the same way: in this corner, people who are adventurous; in that corner, people who are not. Over here, people who are attracted to the new and different; over there, people who feel more comfortable with routine.

And this, too, was a way we'd never lived before.

Cognitive clustering – segregating into sub-groups who think and feel the same way.

This is the origin of *Us vs. Them*.

It began with religions – large clustered groups of people who favor a particular behavioral code, an agreed-upon worldview – in direct opposition to the code and worldview of that *other* group; it spread beyond, inspiring sub-groups of aggressive types who favor taking over dealing, and other sub-groups who found cooperation more emotionally satisfying.

It splintered the human species. After 300,000 years of Nature-enforced cognitive randomization and survival-critical negotiation, we made it possible – by learning to harness edible energy – to split into intellectual and emotional factions. And in that critical step, we ended our innate cooperation and social harmony. We forfeited our inborn humanism, and exchanged it for something less.

These cognitive clusters not only persist today, they're more intense than ever. A half hour of Internet surfing is all it takes to see that our social universe is *driven* by cognitive clustering: our
worldview, our decision-making methods, our beliefs and convictions, all of these derive from the cognitive cluster – the emotionally concentrated tribe – to which we are committed.

What do those clusters look like?

Back in "The Needs of the Many", we looked at the ingredients of cognitive social diversity – the ACC, the insular cortex, the amygdala, and dopamine receptivity (the main ingredients, but certainly not the only ones). And we looked at an example of how variety in these brain components leads to diverse, survival-enhancing social function ('Chuck' and 'Roger').

Cognitive Types

Different combinations of brain components affecting social cognition lead to explicit cognitive types – people who predictably see the world in a similar way, who regard others in a similar way, who possess similar emotional responses – adding up to a shared worldview. Based on the functions and interactions of those brain parts, we can begin to see familiar patterns emerging to form those cognitive types.

And those types are built out of social behaviors we know well, from our own behavior and from what we observe in those around us.

Authoritarian <-> Egalitarian. Authoritarian/Egalitarian is an axis of social cognition, a scale with many points, one of which applies to each of us as an individual. Authoritarianism – the need to outsource decisions (and sometimes beliefs, and sometimes even thought itself) to an alpha, a leader – exists in all of us to some degree: almost all of us will submit to a judge, when we recognize the judge's authority; almost all of us will pull over when flashing lights appear in our rear view mirror.

But some of us are more Authoritarian than others.

Conversely, there is the social impulse to decide jointly – to work with others to achieve a consensus on a course of action: Egalitarianism. We are all egalitarian to some degree, if in nothing more than choosing a restaurant when traveling with a group.

But some of us are more Egalitarian than others.

We all fall somewhere on this social scale, depending largely on our brain parts – and, of course, on our positive and negative social experiences. How Authoritarian/Egalitarian we are as an individual is a big part of how we see others, how we respond to social decisions and challenges, and what emotions we experience in interacting with others.

Threat-Scanning <-> Opportunity-Scanning. Another axis of social cognition is our sensitivity to Risk – another factor determined largely by our personal biology. Some of us are comfortable with taking risks, in the physical world or the social environment; some of us avoid it at all costs; and many fall somewhere in between.

The risk-averse among us scan for threats; the risk-friendly scan for opportunity. Again, we all are at least a little threat-scanning; few are comfortable walking into a dark alley. And we are all at least a little opportunity-conscious; we are pretty receptive, for instance, to free food.

But some are more risk-averse than others; and some are more opportunity-conscious than others.

Novelty-Seeking <-> Uniformity-Seeking. Finally, there is our innate level of openness to the new-and-different, versus our comfort level with the familiar. Many among us love the unexpected, thriving on novel experience – while others find satisfaction in sticking close to what they know well. Again, it's all in the brain, all in the genes, tempered by experience.

And, again, we're all novelty-seekers to some degree: getting to know a new romantic partner is exciting to most all of us, for example. And we all find at least some comfort in what we know – few could tolerate drifting the globe, from one culture to another, being given no time to acclimate in any one place.

Some are more novelty-seeking than others, as others are more uniformity-seeking.

What behaviors and worldviews do we tend to find familiar when we are around people who clearly favor one end or the other of these scales? And where in the brain do those tendencies originate?

An Authoritarian is predisposed to outsource belief and decision-making to a person they perceive to be stronger and more capable than themselves, someone they believe will protect them. This causes them to be distrustful of authorities other than the Leader, and to consider such other-leaders enemies. This predisposition's great evolutionary value was its rapid-response mechanism when the entire tribe was suddenly threatened. Attention is directed by the Leader. Persons with a large amygdala and high dopamine receptivity tend to have this predisposition.

An Egalitarian is one who is boundary-transparent with respect to the tribe. Such a person assigns value to all others of their kind, whether intimate or not, and tends not to outsource belief or decision-making, trusting consensus. This makes them incautious with respect to Others who actually do present danger, but on the other hand they are master integrators of old and new information, making them excellent at long-term planning, for the good of the tribe. Attention tends to roam free.

Persons with larger ACC and insula, along with a smaller amygdala, fit this predisposition.

A *Threat-Scanner* is one whose threshold for risk and perception of danger are lower than average. They spot threats quickly, even to the point of seeing them when they aren't really there. Their value to the tribe is considerable, as they are the first to see real danger and sound the alarm. Because their disposition is impulsive, they are good at immediate decision-making. On the downside, they tend to take a default position of Threat against those not in their tribe. Attention is truncated, in times of threat, to the threat. Persons with a large amygdala and a smaller anterior cingular cortex and insula tend to have this predisposition.

An *Opportunity-Scanner* is one who does not have a strong Threat response, along with a high threshold for negative sensory stimuli. This person is excellent at discovery - finding food, tracking game, studying weather patterns. They can be insensitive to danger and risk, so their social value is that they are able to provide food for the tribe, but they can be reckless. Attention tends to drift from tribal preoccupations. Persons with a larger anterior cingulate cortex and a smaller amygdala tend to have this predisposition.

A *Novelty-Seeker* is one who not only does not mind change, but thrives on it. This person is a superb pattern detector, a master of "One of these things is not like the others." Like the Opportunity Seeker, this person can spot resources and value where others cannot - but rather than simply being less risk-averse, with a propensity for discovery, they are explorers, deliberately pushing across boundaries. In the modern world, such people become artists, writers, musicians, and scientists. Attention is practically random, with a capacity for hyper-focus on objects of curiosity. A combination of small amygdala, low dopamine receptivity, and larger ACC result in this predisposition.

A *Uniformity-Seeker* is a person who feels secure in the familiar. They are slow to accept change and will tend to resist it. They believe there is a Right Way to be and a Right Way to do things. Such persons present tremendous value to the tribe as archivists of What Works, the couriers of knowledge to the next generation - ritualists, traditionalists. They are overly distrustful of new information or voices that challenge their idea of What Works. Attention tends to be limited to those things within the known. Persons with high dopamine receptivity and a smaller ACC tend to have this predisposition.

Add these axes together and you have a social framework defining a subset of the human population. Every combination out there describes a group that we would all find familiar.

Egalitarian/Opportunity-Scanning/Novelty-Seeking

As we discussed earlier, the Paleolithic version of this person is a hunter, a person with great skill as a pattern-finder, able to navigate complex terrain, track difficult prey, forecast changes in the weather – all essential skills for group survival.

In the modern world, this person is an artist or a writer, questing for patterns in the human experience – creative, able to see what others cannot – and prefers to contribute to decisions affecting the group. Such people take risks, often to their detriment. They are fine with change, and even look forward to it.

JebelAuthoritarian/Threat-Scanning/Uniformity-Seeking

The Paleolithic version of this person is great in a pinch – able to react very quickly in precarious situations, someone who can be counted on when help is needed quickly. They aren't deliberative or contemplative, but you don't want those qualities when a leopard attacks – you want action.

Today, that person is a fire chief, or a trauma surgeon, or a military field commander. They take orders well and give orders well, and have little patience with those who like to debate the options. They are uncomfortable with risk, and think those who aren't are careless fools; they are uncomfortable with change, especially social change, and resist it strongly.

These are only two of the possible cognitive types that arise from how our brains work, and from the evolutionary travails that crafted them. The take-home point is this: *all* of these persons, with all of these skills, were required for tribal survival in the ancient past. None could last without the others. The lesson is clear:

When we begin to view others thru these lenses, a whole new layer of understanding emerges... more tolerance, more interest in others, a greater appreciation of our diversity.

The problem is, of course, that we're going in exactly the opposite direction.

Cognitive clustering diminishes our natural humanism. It weakens each of us, depriving us of our capacity to empathize with (and treat as equals) those who think differently than we do. It causes us to downgrade the humanity of others beyond our group. It deprives the groups in which we claim membership from the full range of human problem-solving and decision-making skills.

This is easily seen in the world's religions. Each claims to have the definitive take on human nature, as well as the key solutions to human strife. They disagree wildly in these areas, all asserting that they alone are the definitive authority – and are all equally inadequate to either solve the world's problems or correctly describe human beings, because they are, by definition, only able to see humanity from their own restricted point of view: they have deliberately amputated all of those cognitive skills that they themselves have selected out of their groups.

The same is even more true, and painfully so, of political ideologies. The world today is more partisan than ever, with struggles between authoritarian and egalitarian parties throughout the West – each believing they would be best in charge, each believing their answers are the definitive ones, each thinking they have the inside scoop on human nature – and each equally wrong. As the religions have done, our political parties have self-selected themselves into postures of anemic ineffectiveness, eschewing the cognitive potential of those not in their groups; their deep conviction that *they* are right, that their opponents are self-centered, deluded fools, and that defeating them is everything, is edging the world toward disaster.

Not all social groups are cognitive clusters. Often we find ourselves in groups that are necessarily random, where social cognition is concerned.

A class in an educational institution is an example. Students of all cognitive stripe are found in all high school courses, or an exercise class, or in first aid training. A sports team is another – team members might be strength-oriented authoritarians anxious to submit to the will of the coach, or risk-taking novelty-mongers, out to experience new thrills. And a military unit may be the most randomized of all: assignment to a platoon is a process indifferent to one's social biases.

Consider that these are three of our most effective forms of social grouping: they are all either very high in utility, very high in focused performance, or both. Imagine what our more discriminatory forums could accomplish if they followed suit.

Imagine what will happen if they don't.

"The correct use of power feeds creativity. And the misuse of power destroys it."

~Gene Roddenberry

The Conscience of the King

Distortion: The strong will rule over the weak.

"With the first link, the chain is forged. The first speech censored, the first thought forbidden, the first freedom denied, chains us all irrevocably."
~Jean-Luc Picard, "The Drumhead"

In most primate cultures, the alpha male rules.

A single individual, more powerful than his peers, governs the group by means of strength and intimidation, and in the process inculcates fear in others, takes females at will, and enjoys the highest level of privilege – until toppled from power by a superior challenger. So the story goes, among apes and throughout human history.

The assumption is that we naturally conform to this 'alpha' framework of authority.

But if we are more bonobo than chimpanzee, it no longer makes sense; and if we truly are off course, socially – having screwed up millennia of cooperative social order when we ceased to be migratory – then the idea of alpha humans no longer makes sense.

In modern terms, we call this *Authoritarianism*. It is used in both political science (to describe the political orientation of a nation-state) and psychology (to describe the dynamics of leader-and-follower, where authoritarianism is the rule). It does not differ significantly, in social terms, from what we observe in chimpanzees.

And when it took hold of humankind, it took hold big: for many thousands of years, our sociopolitical systems have been far more authoritarian than not.

Authoritarianism strips the individual of self-determination. By centralizing authority in an individual, it strips the group of the benefit of pooled knowledge and decision-making skills. By awarding group rule according to personal power, rather than according to actual leadership merits, it represents a danger to the group that amplifies over time.

The authoritarian regimes that have come and gone over the millennia that human beings have been civilized are countless. Even in the modern era, the age of democracy, authoritarianism continues to rise up, threatening to return us to a sociopolitically captive state.

This couldn't have happened in the Paleolithic. Human survival hinged on multiple axes, not just one: the group required the leadership of a long-term planner, able to anticipate environmental conditions and food supplies months in advance; adept pattern-finders were needed, individuals able to sense weather change and changes in the behavior of prey; and fast-response captains were needed, in moments of sudden attack from predators.

That's not a single leader – that's several, each with a different skill set…a different cognitive style.

Among chimpanzees, authoritarian leadership limits the tribe; it is not able to organize beyond swarming on prey and internal power struggle. It is a constant competition for the top spot, with no attention to the social development of the tribe.

Among the bonobos, leadership is distributed, as it is in democracies. No one individual member of the tribe holds absolute power, and anyone who tries is rapidly slapped down.

Put simply: when we enabled authoritarianism, we were stepping backward, not forward – and we created a danger that threatens us today, possibly more than it ever has before.

"People judge other people on such superficial grounds that they are very quick to call someone a hypocrite when they come up against a side of them they haven't seen before or are not equipped to deal with. I've been called a hypocrite on flimsier ground than even that - because I saw two sides of an issue when someone wanted me to see one."

~Gene Roddenberry

Family

Distortion: Human beings are self-oriented, not group-oriented.

E.O. Wilson notes that human beings are part of one of the smallest clubs in the kingdom of life. We are a *eusocial* species – one with the nearly-unique trait of sacrificing some measure of personal reproductive potential in order to facilitate the greater goal of group survive.[35]

Wilson notes, with some fascination and astonishment, that only 20 such species have been discovered thus far. And with the exception of a crustacean or two and a mole-rat, all the rest besides us are… insects.

Eusociality is the highest, most sophisticated level of social organization, making a specious largely impervious to the forces that might lead to extinction. Eusocial insect colonies, it is certain, will outlast *Homo sapiens* by hundreds of millions of years, even projecting our best possible species outcomes. What is curious is how we, upright mammals, have come to achieve this heightened state of being, which is largely the province of bugs.

Eusocial species are master cooperators. They are hyper-efficient food gatherers, rabid self-defenders, astonishingly skilled at all the components of survival. Their division of labor is brilliant, highly effective. And they take an extra evolutionary step that bolsters their group survival even more: they care for one another's young.

---

[35] Some biologists contest Wilson's assertion, noting that the other eusocial species all have reproductive and non-reproductive divisions of labor; Wilson counters that this division need not be absolute, but can be a matter of degree.

The role of cooperation in the evolutionary story has been under study for some time - but it is not as well-understood as the role competition, for a simple reason: Nature provides far fewer examples of it. Among many species, it's every creature for itself; among many, it's just a travel buddy thing; even among mammals, many peacefully share territory, but the daily business of eating and sleeping and reproducing isn't considered group activity. It's far more common to see competition, aggression, fighting and fleeing and so on than it is to see the well-ordered community of an insect colony.

Here's the thing: if we look at cooperation as the antithesis of competition, we realize something unsettling: *without* their magnificent cooperation, eusocial insects would be astonishingly vulnerable.

They would be individually much weaker, much more fragile, much more exposed – much less able to draw sustenance from the world. And that's not the unsettling part…

…*so would we.*

An individual human being alone in the world is orders of magnitude more vulnerable than a human in a clan of humans. We are far slower than most other mammals. We are not armed with claws or fangs. We can no longer climb as we once did.

And the ingenuity we innately feel in the here-and-now? That's a heritage from hundreds of thousands of years of ingenuity, handed to us by… the group. Without it, we would flounder in the wild.

But put human beings into eusocial groups, and… *wow.* One human against a leopard is cat food. Six humans against a leopard, the leopard is the food.

Moreover, our infant survival rate skyrockets when we bind into large families. Out in the wild, adoption is rare: most infants will die if their parents die. Among humans, that almost never happens.

And that we care for one another's young has led us to care for one another; we have a power transcending all other eusocial species – empathy. When another of our kind hurts, we hurt; when another feels pleasure, we feel pleasure.

It is not a great leap to see that cooperation is more than just an alternative to competition – it is the next step. Having jumped species, from insect to primate, cooperation can now take Life where competition could not.

It falls to us now, to choose the one over the other. It falls to us now, to choose the one over the other.

Morg and Eymorg

Distortion: Males are naturally superior to females.

As far back as written human history goes, women have been subordinate to men, we noted earlier.

The key words, of course, are "as far back as human history goes," because we also noted earlier that our genes and the architecture of both our bodies and our more innate behaviors indicate that we weren't always this way.

Male dominance of females is relatively new in the human story. Though we see it in many primate species – most uncomfortable, the chimpanzee – we do *not* see it in the species most like ourselves, the bonobo.

Even so, our behaviors since we left behind our carefree days of hunting and gathering have been disturbingly chimpanzee-like: males have, for millennia, decided how and when and under what circumstances mating rights to females would be dispensed and administered – sometimes by authoritarian edict, most often by way of religion.

The patriarchal religions have treated women overtly as property, as far back as written history goes. Women have been taken as spoils of war, offered as payment of debt by their fathers, placed in arranged marriages for political and business purposes, and generally been given neither a voice in their own destiny nor self-determination in their reproductive or personal sexual choices.

The Enlightenment did nothing to change this. Looking back even a few hundred years, we find almost no women among the voices of science, mathematics, philosophy or literature. It is only since the days of our great-grandparents' great-grandparents that we have seen female names on the covers of novels. It is only since the days our great-grandparents that we've seen women with the letters "Dr" preceding their names or the letters "PhD" following them. It is only in those days that they have had the right to vote.

And it is only in our parents' days that women were granted reproductive self-determination, or even the right to own a credit card.

Over the past few decades, there has been rapid progress, but it is far less than women should have been enjoying for millennia.

Even beneath these formal recognitions, there exists a not-very-subtle social bias pervading the simplest day-to-day interactions: an aggressive man is a go-getter, a sure-first success; an aggressive woman is a bitch who needs to be put in her place.

We've already talked about what we owe the human female, for her astonishing contributions to the evolution of our species. The degree to which we've lost our way, where woman is concerned, is difficult to fully describe.

"The acquisition of wealth is no longer the driving force of our lives. We work to better ourselves and the rest of humanity."

~Picard, *Star Trek: First Contact*

Is There in Truth No Beauty?

In summary…
We domesticated plants and animals for food. We settled by the river.
And with this step, we unleashed many demons:

- The concept of 'property' emerged, and with it, 'inheritance';
- Social groups began to divide into hierarchical classes;
- Groups expanded in population, and within the groups, sub-groups began self-segregate according to cognitive type;
- Women became property;
- Threat-Scanning began to grow beyond its evolutionary function – we began to invent dangers out of social fantasies;
- Social dominance came into being, and powerful, manipulative tribal leadership replaced the wisdom of the group;
- We learned to ostracize;
- Bigotry and racism emerged;
- We invented war;
- We lost our common purpose.

Welcome to the 21st century.

"I have a great fear that our human leaders will fail to understand that a world such as Star Trek *is possible - that all the glorious things, not that* Star Trek *represents, but that the human being represents - will fall on deaf ears. That frightens me. There's always a chance that not enough humans will understand and appreciate themselves enough to make a great change in the human equation."*

~Gene Roddenberry

"We may quarrel with Mister Oxmyx's methods, but his goal is essentially the correct one; this society must become united, or it will degenerate into total anarchy."

~Spock, in 'A Piece of the Action'

Return to Tomorrow:

The Restored Human Future

"In diversity, you can trace certain properties of the human spirit that transcend differences. It is only when you look at what unites humans rather than what divides them that you have some idea of what it means to be human."

~ Gene Roddenberry

Infinite Diversity in Infinite Combinations

Restored: Diversity, in mind and form, restores the path to evolutionary success...

Before Kirk, Spock and Uhura stands a being in the image of Abraham Lincoln, a personal hero of Kirk's. In the course of their exchange, 'Lincoln' fears he has offended Uhura – by calling her a 'charming Negress'.

"But why should I object to that term, sir?" Uhura asks. "You see, in our century, we've learned not to fear words."

"The foolishness of my century had me apologizing where no offense was given," Lincoln replies.

Kirk sums it up: "We've each learned to take delight in what we are. The Vulcans learned that centuries before we did."

Infinite Diversity, in Infinite Combinations - IDIC. It is a guiding principle of Vulcan philosophy, the center of their value system. *Kol-Ut-Shan*[36] in the native tongue, it celebrates differences in-kind and beyond, and is part of their historical path to universal peace.

---

[36] From "Gravity," *Star Trek: Voyager.*

We first saw the IDIC – a medallion reflecting the concept – in the episode "Is There in Truth No Beauty?", hanging around Spock's neck at a dinner honoring Dr. Miranda Jones, a human telepath preparing to mind-meld with a very non-human Medusan. Spock connects the medallion to the philosophy: "The triangle and the circle - different shapes, materials, textures - represent any two diverse things which come together to create here, truth or beauty."

Though Gene Roddenberry created the medallion so he'd have a new toy to sell to fans, the philosophy of IDIC was a winner with the cast, the crew, and everyone in the *Star Trek* universe. It perfectly embodies the humanist theme of the show.

"Infinite Diversity in Infinite Combinations represents a Vulcan belief that beauty, growth, progress, all result from the union of the unlike. Concord, as much as discord, requires the presence of at least two different notes," Roddenberry explained. "The brotherhood of man is an ideal based on learning to delight in our essential differences, as well as learning to recognize our similarities. The circle and triangle combine to produce the gemstone in the center as the union of words and music creates song, or the union of marriage creates children."[37]

And it can honestly be said that Roddenberry's attitude toward diversity was present from the start, evident in his eventual casting of the show, with its multinational crew. It's a statement that is apparent to any viewer in their first few moments of watching any episode, a statement that persisted through all of *Trek*'s on-screen incarnations.

But it's about more than variety in skin color and culture: diversity lurks deep beneath our surface – and is perhaps more survival-critical than any other aspect of humanism.

The Ancient Human IDIC

But diversity is more than a key to future harmony and growth. Diversity was, ironically, the key to human survival, when we were genetically at our most Homogenous.

Confined in our earlier millennia to Central Africa, we had not yet developed the broad range of skin tones we now enjoy; our culture in particular was decidedly monotone, as we had not yet developed writing, art, or even language.

Yet we had already begun experiencing the most important diversity of all: differences in thought.

---

[37] Quoted in *Inside Star Trek*, by Herbert Solow and Robert Justman, p. 15.

By this, we aren't thinking of differences in philosophies or doctrines or ideologies like those that surround us today – those things didn't yet exist. We're talking about *literal* differences in thought – the actual variations that existed (and still exist!) in human brains, diversity in proportional quantities of brain tissue in different brain regions – diversity that resulted (and still does today) in some variation in how each of us processes the world.

We've looked at those brain variations themselves, and how different combinations of brain components resulted in different cognitive contributions to tribal survival. And we've considered how destructive it is when that cognitive diversity is dampened when humans cluster together in cults of like-mindedness. Now let's look at the evidence.

Diversity Makes Us Smarter

"Great things in business are never done by one person. They're done by a team of people."

~Steve Jobs

Scientific American gathered together summaries of a number of studies demonstrating the advantages of diversity in the workplace,[38] concluding that being around people who think differently increases our creativity and diligence.

Cristian Deszö of the University of Maryland and David Ross of Columbia University, for instance, noted the impact of gender diversity in business. Reviewing the size and gender make-up of the top equity firms from 1992-2006, they found that, on average, firms with women in top management positions demonstrated greater financial performance than those without. Orlando Richard of the University of Texas found in a 2003 study that the same holds true for racial diversity in upper management.

A 2006 study at the University of Illinois teamed subjects to solve a murder mystery exercise, varying the racial make-up of the three-person teams. Teams with a non-white member significantly out-performed all-white teams.

Another University of Illinois study in 2013 tasked subjects to identify as either Democrat or Republican, then read a murder mystery and decide who they thought committed the crime. They were then tasked to write an essay making their case, for presentation to another test subject in hopes of convincing them. Half of the subjects were told they would be making the

---

[38] In *Scientific American*, Oct. 2014.

case to a member of their own political party; half were told they'd be trying to convince a member of the other party. Subjects of both parties prepared less well and wrote a less persuasive essay when they believed they were going to be talking to a member of their own party. "Diversity jolts us into cognitive action in ways that Homogeneity simply does not," the study concluded.

And in 2014, Richard Freeman and Wei Huang of Harvard University examined ethnicity among the authors of 1.5 million scientific papers, noting that those written by ethnically diverse research teams received more citations than those written by teams of people with common ethnicity.

Finally there's a 2006 study by Samuel Sommers of Tufts University, where real judges, jury administrators and jurors participated in a mock jury experiment to determine the effects of racial diversity in jury decision-making. Sommers arranged the jurors into all-white groups and four-white, two-black groups. The diverse juries made fewer errors in recall of important information and discussed the role of race in the case more openly. Sommers concluded that in the presence of diversity, white jurors "were more diligent and open-minded," according to *Scientific American*.

Cognitive diversity and performance

But gender, race, and political orientation, though qualifying as diversity, do not necessarily imply *cognitive* diversity. In an article in the *Harvard Business Review*,[39] Alison Reynolds and David Lewis took up the problem, using Peter Robertson's AEM Cube tool[40] to assess a person's knowledge processing and perspective in new situations.

Six teams were created, variable in their degree of AEM Cube ratings, and were then given a group task to complete. The teams with greater diversity in knowledge processing and perspective completed the exercise more quickly; the greater the level of diversity, the higher the team's score.

Reynolds and Lewis further noted that cognitive diversity is a more reliable performance enhancer than gender and racial diversity, comparing the AEM Cube study to other performance studies:

[39] "Teams Solve Problems Faster When They're Cognitively Diverse," March 30, 2017

[40] The AEM Cube is an assessment tool that measures three axes of personality: Attachment, Exploration, and Managing contribution (approach to complexity). It is called a "cube" because the results can be mapped to three-dimensional space.

"Someone being from a different culture or a different generation gives no clue as to how that person might process information, engage with, or respond to change," they wrote. "We cannot easily detect cognitive diversity from the outside. It cannot be predicted or easily orchestrated. The very fact that it is an internal difference requires us to work hard to surface it and harness the benefits."

Cognitive diversity aboard the *Enterprise*

Though Roddenberry may not have been thinking of it at the time, the bridge of the *Enterprise* gives us yet another example of the merits of cognitive diversity: it is difficult to imagine two people whose information processing styles differ more than Spock and McCoy, and the stylistic disparity is greater still when the rest of the bridge officers are added to the mix. Yet the Integration of these differences is what informs Kirk's decisions and viewpoint, time and again.

Vonda McIntyre's *Trek* novel *Enterprise: The First Adventure* (1987) takes an interesting turn here: when Kirk is first given command, the admiral giving it to him rejects his choice of his best friend, Gary Mitchell, as first officer, insisting that Spock, who has served on the ship for years under Captain Christopher Pike, be promoted into the role. The admiral's argument is that Kirk and Mitchell are too much alike, and that both Kirk and the crew will benefit from a command team with greater differences.

Finally, we have the words of Surak, the father of Vulcan philosophy, spoken to Kirk later in "The Savage Curtain":

> "In my time, we knew not of Earthmen. I am pleased to see that we have differences. May we together become greater than the sum of both of us."

"The strength of a civilization is not measured by its ability to fight wars, but rather by its ability to prevent them."

~ Gene Roddenberry

The Inner Light

Restored: Human beings inevitably think
differently, as they should, and always will...

More than a hundred delegates from an assortment of Federation worlds crowd the Enterprise, *bound for the neutral planetoid codenamed Babel, there to address the politically charged question of admitting Coridan to the Federation – a planet rich with coveted resources, ripe for plunder, in need of the protection of Federation law.*

Among the delegates – Humans of Earth; the stoic Vulcans; the volatile Tellarites; the cold Andorians, and many others, forming a strong and varied mix of perspectives, thinking styles, and temperaments – the mix that enables the Federation in the first place.

The consequences of cognitive clustering are many. Even the list covered so far in these chapters doesn't cover them all. Almost every social stumble humankind has made can be traced back to this deeply destructive aberration.

But as deep as this divisive tendency has sliced, its reversal can have deeper impact still. When we look around and survey our addiction to like-mindedness, admit that it is social kryptonite, and commit to the brain-building, community-building work of *de*-clustering our lives, our groups, and our world, the rewards are beyond enticing – they are species-changing.

The person who commits to seeking out groups that are cognitively varied is inviting debate, uncertainty, some self-doubt, and certainly some opposition – but will be rewarded with deeper perspective, more thoroughly tested convictions, stronger self-expression, and a more rewarding understanding of human nature.

The group that commits to cognitive inclusion, setting aside its echo-chamber dynamic to invite differing viewpoints, new styles of thought, and opposing voices, will be rewarded with more reliable decision-making resources, a far greater range of problem-solving skills, a more viable and effective presence in the world, and a deeper and more rewarding diversity in its ranks.

This is certainly more easily said than done. In the West, cognitive clustering is the default. Most of us live in echo chambers, often inherited from our parents – and the Internet has amplified that effect, rather than pushing back against it.

It is certainly more immediately gratifying to just seek out that little dopamine hit we get when we have a beer with friends and commiserate together, nodding and agreeing with each other, than it is to sit down with those we disagree with – or even despise – and do the hard work of setting aside our emotional opposition to their viewpoint in order to see what it is that motivates them and moves them. It's hard to believe that the eat-your-vegetables labor of cognitive de-clustering can ultimately be as rewarding as making cultural war on those who see the world, and even the human race, differently.

But those of us in the United States, our current dysfunction aside, have a model to work with – one that puts us, in our self-serving attitude, to shame.

Our Founding Founders, our Constitutional Framers, sought to instill *exactly* this form of social action, this same cognitively varied dynamic.

The *entire point* of this thing we call the United States is a cognitively diverse, de-clustered forum for problem-solving and decision-making. The Constitution's mechanics specifically enforce the kind of work-the-problem deliberation, uniting deliberators of diverse background and viewpoint in the service of building the nation and addressing its issues. In short, the Founders' secular, intellectually unbiased style of government achieves the humanist ideal – and provides the template we need, a framework for returning human society to its lost state of social health – diverse in body and mind, strong in problem-solving, deep in its self-understanding, and far-reaching in its perception of the possibilities of the future.

It becomes a matter of personal commitment to individual action, which in turn brings the committed into encounter with one another, not only tolerating but welcoming those who are different – entering into a growing sphere of diverse groups, each composed of strong and perceptive members, able to cope well with adversity, disagreement, the labors of consensus-building, the challenges of solving troubling problems and the satisfactions of complicated decisions faced and well-made.

It is not a trivial commitment. In the end, it is at least as serious as joining a church or a political party, and demands at least as much (if not far more). It is a lonelier path, a road less traveled.

But there is no other path to Babel.

"It is the confrontation with evil that is good, not the avoidance of it."

~Gene Roddenberry

Let That Be Your Last Battlefield

Restored: Peace.

"Yes, Councilman, you have a real war on your hands. You can either wage it with real weapons, or you might consider an alternative. Put an end to it. Make peace."
~Kirk, to Anan 7, in the conflict between Eminiar VII and Vendikar

In his 2012 book *The End of War*, science writer John Horgan tells of Wesleyan University's David Adams, a psychologist who polled his students in the 1980s, asking them what they thought about war. The results were discouraging. Almost one-third answered "Yes" when asked whether "wars are inevitable because human beings are naturally aggressive" - and an even more discouraging 40 percent said "Yes" to the statement "War is intrinsic to human nature."

Horgan reported that Adams had written, "These results support the need for a worldwide educational campaign to dispel the myth that war is instinctive, intrinsic to human nature, or unavoidable because of an alleged biological bias.

Horgan reported further that Adams and 19 colleagues met in Spain in 1986, in a conference sponsored by the United Nations, to present the following five propositions:

1. It is scientifically incorrect to say that we have inherited a tendency to make war from our animal ancestors;

2. It is scientifically incorrect to say that war or any other violent behavior is genetically programmed into our human nature;
3. It is scientifically incorrect to say that in the course of human evolution there has been a selection for aggressive behavior more than for other kinds of behavior;
4. It is scientifically incorrect to say that humans have a "violent brain";
5. It is scientifically incorrect to say that war is caused by "instinct" or any single motivation.

The Seville Statement, as it was called, wrapped up by stating "that biology does not condemn humanity to war, and that humanity can be freed from the bondage of biological pessimism... the same species who invented war is capable of inventing peace. The responsibility lies within each of us.

After building the case that war is a choice, that resource scarcity is no excuse, and that the correct view of war is as a cultural contagion, Horgan presents his vision for the end of war, offering a handful of universal rules:

- Indiscriminate killing, of the sort that happens when mines, bombs and drones are used, must be ruled out;
- The highest priority in conflict between nations must be the minimization of civilian casualties (Horgan suggests that the de-escalation policies commonly adopted by police be used as a model);
- Any armed aggression between nation should be architected in such a way as to occur its own obsolescence (long-term consequences should be the highest consideration).

And finally, Horgan underscores his thesis with a recap of the "Prehistory of Violence," much of which we've already reviewed. His recaps include the following:

- 20,000 years ago: oldest skeleton bearing uncontested indications (an arrowhead in the body, among other things) of homicide, discovered in the Nile Valley;
- 13,000 years ago: the oldest mass grace, Cemetery 117 (see "A Private Little War", page 32);

- 10,000 years ago: "irrefutable evidence" of organized warfare discovered in northern Mesopotamia, including spears and arrow points, fortifications, and bones with signs of violence.

The point: the appearance of organized warfare in human prehistory was both abrupt and recent. There are no mass graves dating back into the Paleolithic, no patterns of bone damage, no stockpiles of weapons. There is an overwhelming abundance of evidence of human cooperation – and none of systemic aggression.

War is a recent innovation. And John Horgan, Douglas Fry, and Raymond Kelly, among others, believe it can be banished forever.

But what about peace? What is its true history in the human adventure, and how do we bring it forth permanently?

Douglas Fry, in his book *The Human Potential for Peace*, quotes Charles Darwin in *The Descent of Man*:

> "No tribe could hold together if murder, robbery,
> treachery, etc., were common; consequently such crimes
> within the limits of the same tribe 'are branded
> with everlasting infamy;'"

He also quotes anthropologist Brian Ferguson[41]:

> "The image of humanity, warped by bloodlust,
> inevitably marching off to kill, is a powerful myth and
> an important prop of militarism in our society. Despite
> its lack of scientific credibility, there will remain those
> 'Hard-headed realists' who continue to believe in it,
> congratulating themselves for their 'courage to face the
> truth,' resolutely oblivious to the myth behind their
> 'reality'."

And back to Darwin:

> "As man advances in civilization, and small tribes are
> united into larger communities, the simplest reason
> would tell each individual that he ought to extend his

---

[41] In "Introduction: Studying War", *Warfare, Culture, and Environment*, Academic Press, 1984.

social instincts and sympathies to all the other members
of the same nation, though personally unknown to him.
This point being once reached, there is only an
rtificial barrier to prevent his sympathies extending to
the men of all nations and races."

Fry invests considerable effort in articulating case studies of peaceful behaviors among aboriginal groups, detailing their conflict management practices, and demonstrating the utility and portability of those practices. He also examines a broad range of social organization paradigms, weighing the quality of each in maintaining peace.

Frans de Waal provides a biological foundation for a key component of peaceful coexistence – reconciliation behaviors – in Thomas Gregor's *A Natural History of Peace*.

He begins by providing three evolutionary mechanisms by which aggression is controlled in primate groups: Risk of Injury/Energy Expenditure; Memory of Prior Defeats/Injuries; and Value of Cooperation/Threat to Group Membership.

He then frames his argument by evaluating two competing hypotheses regarding the effects of aggression on social relations. The first is a *dispersal hypothesis*, which predicts that losers would socially avoid winners, the second is a *reconciliation hypothesis*, which predicts that individuals will attempt to repair relationships to restore social value. He and his team then tested the two hypotheses through observation of a range of different primates, capturing patterns of reconciliation.

His finding was that both patterns are frequently displayed: dispersal is commonplace following aggressive confrontation, but reconciliation will follow after a brief period of time.

Anthropologist Leslie Sponsel, also writing in *A Natural History of Peace*, makes the case that social mechanisms for implementing peace as a global default already exist, summarizing:

"Humans have evolved both biological and cultural
behavioral mechanisms to promote nonviolence and
peace as well as to avoid, reduce, and resolve conflict
and violence. Indeed ethnography does provide *heuristic
precedents and models* of sociocultural systems that are
relatively nonviolent and peaceful."

Economist Kenneth Boulding, in the same volume, builds a case for global peace as an inevitable emergent feature of *adaptive learning*, as the nations of the world face an increasing stream of unique challenges. He also offers the optimistic reminder that peace is now a formal research topic:

"...we are looking for a dialectics of learning rather than a dialectics of struggle. One of the hopeful signs emerging from this search has been the development of the peace-research movement of the last 30 or 40 years, which essentially defines peace as creative conflict and a learning process as over against the old dialectic that cannot live without an enemy."

This was, in fact, the theme *Trek* writer/director Nicholas Meyer was attempting to explore in *Star Trek VI: The Undiscovered Country*, in which Captain Kirk is forced to confront his own prejudices against the Klingons and his desire to achieve retribution for the murder of his son David.

"'I need my enemy to define me,'" Meyer summarized, then explaining that the point of Kirk's confrontation with the Klingons is ultimately to rise above that need. Though this plotline didn't go down very well with those fans who believed that, per Roddenberry's vision, Kirk should already have been there, the movie had the virtue of presenting a Klingon chancellor as the source of wisdom and inspiration in the pursuit of ultimate peace between the Federation and Klingon Empire. That in itself was a step forward long overdue.

And that's a part of the *Trek* future that can become real.

Best of Both Worlds

Restored: Male and female are different, but equal...

We came out of the trees together. We walked on two legs and roamed the land and survived together. We developed equally large and capable brains together, tamed fire together, became tool users together. We gave rise to 10,000 generations of our kind as we marched, hand in hand, to the edge of civilization.

Then we parted, male and female – males taking power, females reduced to property.

The injustice of this is presumed, in many corners of the world today and in the minds of hundreds of millions. But progress in restoring women to their true place in the human story, where they not only flourish but guide and lead, rather than serve and follow, has been slow in coming.

The course into the human future is a course navigated by woman and man in full partnership, each giving of the best of their many gifts. It isn't enough to make this a matter of properly distributed authority and just dispensation of social rights; it must be a matter of individual commitment to the practical ideal of gender equality, earnest appreciation of the diversity that our differences bring forth.

It must be a matter of mutual forgiveness, for our individual errors in both understanding and behavior and our collective errors in social practice – not only a matter of shared policy, but an accepted responsibility for all.

Finally, it's must be a matter of constant awareness: if we're to bring about a fully human future, leaving no one behind, we face several transitional generations that will require vigilance and sensitivity on the part of men, who can try but never fully succeed in seeing the world as their sisters do: for though not all men have mistreated or failed to appreciate women, all women have been, at one time or another, mistreated or unappreciated by a man.

And the Children Shall Lead

Restored: Human young are raised by the group.

Carrying a little girl, Kirk – bloodied, uniform in tatters - leads Jaun and Miri back through the dilapidated maze of corridors to the lab where Spock and the others wait – and McCoy is lying on the floor, unconscious, full of a tenuous antidote to a virus that is killing them all. McCoy's blisters fade; the antidote works.

"Is this a good thing, Miri?" Jaun asks Miri.

Now the children will age normally and live. They have endured endless years alone together, with only each other to rely on. Jaun and Miri and the other older children will help the younger children grow and learn, with the help of adults provided by Starfleet, to guide them back to healthy development and a strong society.

Today we box children up and assign one or two adults to provide most of their social and intellectual training. This has been going on for generations.

Tomorrow, we have the opportunity to reintegrate them into society fully, in the way that our ancient ancestors, as growing children, were integrated into theirs.

A return to Dunbar-style community – intimate networks of human beings, living in close proximity and sharing the daily tasks of life and work and family – provides the potential to put growing children not into clusters of peers who share their lack of training and experience, but into groups made up of young and old, learning not from one adult but from many, among children not just of the same age but of all ages.

"It takes a village to raise a child," Hillary Clinton famously wrote, though that bit of wisdom has been around throughout history.

It began in prehistory.

The idea that human beings are naturally monogamous is easily set aside these days. We are all very aware that life-long partnership is very much the exception, rather than the rule. But it's only within the last couple of generations that this has been openly acknowledged, owing to religious propriety.

Monogamy itself, as a human mating practice, is thought to be a very recent innovation in the *Homo sapiens* story, based on genetic studies[42]; polygyny and polyandry were the norms, and we have evidence that women were particularly selective (see page 41), the unconscious architects of gene distribution. This produces a portrait of human families as very extended, with highly-distributed paternity and genetic diversity. For such groups to work, Hillary Clinton's 'village' would have been essential: all adults would have participated in the raising of all children - feeding them, passing on skills, protecting them.

Something closer to this was in fact the familial norm for most of civilized history, as well; while polygyny was generally a privilege hoarded by royalty, extended families were the template for child-rearing for thousands of years, across cultures. Children learned about themselves and others in homes containing three generations or more. The 'nuclear family' we know today – two generations, two adults, with one or more children created by the two adults – is a family structure that has only been around for about 25 generations, first appearing in Europe.[43]

Put another way, we'd been doing it right all along – until we started doing it wrong.

---

[42] "A recent shift from polygyny to monogamy is suggested by the analysis of worldwide Y-chromosome diversity," I. Dupanloup et al, *Journal of Molecular Evolution* 57(1), 85-97.

[43] Per historians Alan Macfarlane and Peter Laslett.

Michael Tomasello, in his book *Becoming Human*, presents a theory of ontogeny [44] that informs our discussion of human prehistory. In a nutshell, he has identified features of development in human children that underscores the thesis that *Homo sapiens* is genetically predisposed to cooperation and to self-organize cognition around social norms and behaviors.

According to Tomasello, human children naturally progress through three crucial stages of cognitive development that shape her mind to cooperate, empathize, and optimize its social cognition features:

- The first stage occurs around nine months, during which the child begins to practice *joint intentionality*, which Tomasello defines as a condition including "two individuals who have a joint goal, structured by joint attention, each of whom has at the same time her own individual role and perspective"; Tomasello states that children begin to practice this joint intentionality with caregivers; this joint intentionality is the cornerstone of cooperation;
- The second stage happens around age three, at which time a child will begin practicing *collective intentionality* - perceiving themselves as part of a group of peers, responding to authoritative adults, responding to instruction, accepting cultural input, and observing/imitating the behaviors of co-equals;
- The third stage emerges around age six or seven, and a child becomes less reliant on adult regulation in the formation of social behaviors and beliefs about the world, and more inclined to self-regulate.

Tomasello's model describes a brain development that enables and coincides with moral development, cultivating not just cooperation, but a framework for the interdependence that underlies human morality (see "How Morality Evolved", page 68). It ties the essential human inclination to cooperative, moral behavior not to reasoning or social structures or innovation, but to the natural development of a child's mind.

And it's here that we can begin optimizing for the future, by creating environments beyond the limitations of the nuclear family and a production-oriented educational systems – environments that give children to a wider range of more emotionally-engaged caregivers,

---

[44] *Ontogenesis* refers to the development of an organism from its earliest stage to maturity.

structured to make Tomasello's three stages much more enriched and diverse.

*"I think that humans are incredible - they are
the most fascinating things
in the universe."*

~Gene Roddenberry

To Summon the Future

Restored: Humanity united in common purpose.

Common purpose.

When human beings unite to pursue a common goal – when every member of the group is committed to that goal, and the group resolves to stand or fall together – we are at our very strongest. This brand of unity guided us through hundreds of thousands of years of evolutions; it can guide us to the stars.

Are the stars our destination? Almost any *Trek* fan you could find would say, unequivocally, "Yes!!!" They may be, but then again, they may not; both the How and the Why of interstellar travel on a *Star Trek* scale are problematic, and worthy of careful consideration.

Whether our goal is the stars or something else, we all need to seek it together. It's the commitment to a common destiny that binds humanity in such a way that we don't turn on ourselves. It was the dissipation of our shared survival imperative, in a new world of settlements and crops and stratified social classes and agendas and objectives, that opened the Pandora's Box of inequality, greed, and conflict.

A common purpose needs objectives that can be shared throughout the group, and rewards that can likewise benefit all.

Those purposes we have in abundance – and two stand out.

- *We have a planet in peril*, suffering increasingly toxic atmosphere and oceans;
- *We, as a species, prey upon ourselves*. This not only needs to stop, it must be reversed; human life should cease to be disposable, and become revered – the one thing in the universe infinitely worth preserving, protecting, and

developing. The smallest child among us should come to be
seen as of greater value than the richest man's fortune.

Can we agree that if we choose to pursue the stars, we stand little
chance of getting there – or, for that matter, doing anything of meaning
when we do – if we fail to heal the one planet in our care, and unite as a
species?

These two things are our top priority. To summon the future, we must
do the difficult work of preparing ourselves to meet it. This eventually
must be a collective commitment – but it must begin with each of us as
individuals. Such a monumental undertaking is necessarily the product of
each one sitting down, counting the cost, and committing to becoming a
positive force, each day, for both humanity and the planet we inhabit.
How? There are countless ways, from environmental activism to social
volunteerism to political action to reform our governments. We can't be
certain, in advance, of which efforts will be fruitful and which won't.

We can only be certain that if each of us doesn't make the commitment
and follow up with daily effort, none of them will happen at all.

The Way to Eden

"And as captain, I want two things done! First, find Cyrano Jones! And second... close that door."

How do we summon the future? How do we get there from here, especially when humanity seems so deeply committed to going in the other direction?

There are a few big things we need to do, but even the big things are made up of little things – things we can all do. The idea is to restore those things we've lost, those traits and behaviors that defined us for hundreds of thousands of years – binding us together, empowering even the least of us, dissipating our selfish and destructive tendencies.

De-clustering. We must stop forming social groups filled with people who all think the same way, and embrace social groups that force us to really understand and work with those who think differently.

Returning to Dunbar. Today, human beings tend to be intimately close to a few other people and very socially distant from all the rest. Tomorrow, we'll be a healthier species if we recommit our social brain space to greater circles of intimacy and close social support,
and by way of our intellect commit to respect for those we don't know well.

Returning the woman to her rightful place. Half of us our female. And at least half of the credit for the rapid development of our species and our survival over the eons goes to the female. Science has spoken (as if we really needed it to), and we know beyond any doubt that anything a man can do, a woman can do at least as well – from discovering an element and performing surgery to writing novels and commanding a starship...

Looking each other in the eye again, and renewing our sense of touch. Our society is deeply impersonal for a reason; our brains aren't wired to deal with the thousands of human beings we encounter every day. Still, our tendency *not* to look one another in the eye is reflexive, and is a defensive measure on the part of our neocortex; we tend to minimize, rather than maximize our contacts with others. In doing so, we deprive ourselves not only of a wealth of information about who they are, their intentions, and the emotions they are trying to convey to us, but we blunt our sensitivity to all of that information across the board. We can consciously overcome that reflex, and know one another more fully – even those with whom our contact is casual.

Fully understanding human nature. Only by studying, in abstract and in practice, the cognitive differences between ourselves and others can we come to a full understanding of human nature as it really is. Our cognitive clusters define 'human being' according to a single, shared model, one that appeals to our particular brain and the brains most like ours; we lose all the richness of the perception of human nature that can be gained from the other cognitive types if we fail to move beyond our own group in an effort to grasp the entire human portrait.

Ex astra, scientia. "From the stars, knowledge." It's the motto of Starfleet. And if you're not a Carl Sagan/Neil deGrasse Tyson fan, now's the time to become one: Earth is all we have, at least for our lifetimes and a good many generations to do – and only by studying the cosmos can we fully appreciate the marvelous planet with which we've been entrusted, an appreciation that can ignite our passion for...

Rediscovering common purpose. We are, as far as we can know today, given the augmented reach of our senses, the pinnacle of intelligence and gift in all the universe – and we have a planet in peril. The salvation of our species and the healing of our world are not only worthy of our very best united efforts – they are essential to our survival. We must discover new ways of thinking, new ways of seeing, new ways of knowing – new ways of living together.

"I have seen much to criticize in mankind. But I believe there's even more to admire."

~Questor

On the Edge of Forever

The Promise of the Human Future

"You know, I couldn't believe it when the bartender told me who you are," Captain Pike tells a bruised and bleeding Jim Kirk.

It's well past midnight in a rural bar near Starfleet's Riverside, Iowa shipyards. An hour earlier, Kirk had his ass handed to him by four cadets, after he drunkenly hit on Nyota Uhura.

"Who am I, Captain Pike?" Kirk asks.

"Your father's son," the captain replies. "For my dissertation, I was assigned the USS Kelvin. Something I admired about your dad: he didn't believe in no-win scenarios."

"Sure learned his lesson," Kirk observes. His father died aboard the Kelvin, making sure the newborn Kirk and his mother could escape.

"Well, it depends on how you define winning. You're here, aren't you?"

Kirk takes another drink.

"You know that instinct to leap without looking, that was his nature, too. And in my opinion, it's something Starfleet's lost."

Kirk laughs at him. "Why are you talkin' to me, man?"

"Because I looked up your file while you were drooling on the floor," Pike answers, now with some urgency. "Your *aptitude tests are off the charts. So what is it? You like being the only genius-level repeat offender in the Midwest?"*

"Maybe I love it."

"Look, so your dad dies," Pike says, looking right at Kirk. "You can settle for a less-than-ordinary life – or do you feel like you were meant for something better? Something special?"

Pike isn't just talking to the 22-year-old, pre-Starfleet Jim Kirk. Those words ring out to the entire human race, here in the early 21st century, as we sit and nurse our latest wounds, wondering over our propensity to find ourselves brawling and none too starry-eyed about tomorrow.

As far as we are able to determine today, we represent the pinnacle of intelligence and accomplishment in the known universe. That being the case, will we accept a less-than-ordinary future?

Or were we meant for something better? Something special?

"Mankind will reach maturity on the day it learns to value diversity - of life and ideas. To be different is not necessarily to be ugly: to have a different idea is not necessarily to be wrong. The worst thing that could happen is for all of us to look and think and act alike. For if we cannot learn to value the small variations among our own kind here on Earth, then God help us when we get out into space and meet the variations that are almost certainly out there."

~Gene Roddenberry

"The human adventure is just beginning..."

A Gene Roddenberry

Appendix I: Some Debate

It will come as no surprise to learn that many of the ideas, claims, and theses above have not achieved full consensus in academic circles, which is very often the case in science. We are less than a generation removed from the Killer Ape theory, and the copious data provided by our closest cousins – the chimp and the bonobo – avails of more than one interpretation.

It should also be noted that there are some heavy hitters among the dissenters. British evolutionary biologist Richard Dawkins is perhaps the best known among them, though Canadian psychologist Steven Pinker is a close second. Neuroendocrinologist Robert Sapolsky, though not a household name, is also a prominent voice who resists some of these ideas.

The Federation credo includes freedom of expression, so their views should, in all fairness, have their moment.

Individual Selection vs. Group Selection

One of the central pillars of the paradigm presented in this book is the idea that natural selection, the foundation of biology, operates beyond the level of the individual. Specifically, there's group selection, the idea that natural selection operates at the group level as well as the individual level, selecting on the basis of traits that promote the survival of the group, not just the individual.

As mentioned above, biologist E.O. Wilson is the pacesetter here: "Within groups, selfish individuals outcompete altruistic ones," he has said, "but altruistic *groups* outcompete selfish ones."

More specifically, he said in his book *Genesis: The Deep Origins of Society*: "Group selection is natural selection of alleles that that prescribe social traits. The traits favored by natural selection are those that entail the interaction of individuals within groups, including the initial formation of the groups. As groups of the same species then compete, the genes of their members are tested, driving social evolution by natural selection up or down. A rich documentation of this process has been provided by both natural history and experimental studies."

Wilson may be the most prominent champion of group selection, but the concept originated with none other than Charles Darwin. In his masterpiece *The Descent of Man*, he wrote:

> "When two tribes of primeval man, living in the same
> country, came into competition, if (other things being
> equal) the one tribe included a great number
> of courageous, sympathetic and faithful members, who
> were always ready to warn each other of danger, to aid
> and defend each other, this tribe would succeed better
> and conquer the other."

Darwin fully understood the implications, anticipating Wilson:

> "It is extremely doubtful whether the offspring of the
> more sympathetic and benevolent parents, or of those
> who were the most faithful to their comrades, would be
> reared in greater numbers than the children of selfish and
> treacherous parents belonging to the same tribe. He who
> was ready to sacrifice his life, as many a savage has
> been, rather than betray his comrades, would often leave
> no offspring to inherit his noble nature."

Darwin aside, however, the theory of group selection has been butting heads very publicly and persistently with individual selection since Wilson's *Sociobiology* was first published in 1975. At the time, it ran afoul with *The Selfish Gene*, Richard Dawkins' cornerstone work, which strongly asserts that it is individual selection that drives evolution, and that the idea of group selection is misguided: the gene reigns supreme in natural selection (that is certainly true), and presents the following argument against group selection:

> "Even in the group of altruists, there will almost
> certainly be a dissenting minority who refuse to make
> any sacrifice. If there is just one selfish rebel, prepared
> to exploit the altruism of the rest, then he, by definition,
> is more likely than they are to survive and have children.
> Each of these grandchildren will tend to inherit his
> selfish traits. After several generations of this natural
> selection, the 'altruistic group will be over-run by selfish

individuals, and will be indistinguishable from the selfish group. Even if we grant the improbable chance existence initially of altruistic groups without any rebels, it is very difficult to see what is to stop selfish individuals migrating in from neighboring selfish groups, and, by inter-marriage, contaminating the purity of the altruistic groups."

Robert Sapolsky has expressed a similar view:

"The old notion of group selection has been proven wildly incorrect. This is the idea that animals behave 'for the good of the species' and that behaviors are driven by ways to increase the likelihood of the species surviving and multiplying. Evolution is not about animals behaving for the good of the species but, rather, behaving to optimize the number of copies of their own genes to pass on to the next generation."

Steven Pinker's position:

"Group selection has become a scientific dust bunny, a hairy blob in which anything having to do with "groups" clings to anything having to do with "selection." The problem with scientific dust bunnies is not just that they sow confusion; … the apparent plausibility of one restricted version of "group selection" often bleeds outwards to a motley collection of other, long-discredited versions. The problem is that it also obfuscates evolutionary theory by blurring genes, individuals, and groups as equivalent levels in a hierarchy of selectional units; ...this is not how natural selection, analyzed as a mechanistic process, really works. Most importantly, it has placed blinkers on psychological understanding by seducing many people into simply equating morality and culture with group selection, oblivious to alternatives that are theoretically deeper and empirically more realistic."

He has also said "Group selection has no useful role to play in psychology or social science... [it] is not a precise implementation of the theory of natural selection, as it is, say, in genetic algorithms or artificial life simulations. Instead it is a loose metaphor, more like the struggle between kinds of tires or telephones."

The disconnect between advocates for both views is that the question is framed as either/or, as opposed to the presentation of a model wherein individual selection and group selection are coexisting components of natural selection. Moreover, individual selectionists commonly misrepresent the position of group selectionists by claiming they wish to replace the unit of selection – the gene – with "group". Group selectionists generally agree that the gene is the unit of selection, but argue for a more complex model: that genes favoring altruistic behaviors are more likely to be replicated more often because the behaviors enhance the group's survival odds.

The question is not yet settled, and may not soon be, but the discussion is a worthy one, and central to questions surrounding our ultimate humanist potential.

The Demonic Male

There remain a number of thinkers in academia who continue to hold variations of the Killer Ape model of paleolithic humanity. Among these are Harvard University's Richard Wrangham[45] and Dale Peterson, who present a portrait of the "demonic male", in which primates are not simply inherently violent, but murderous. They base their argument on the commonalities in violent patterns of behavior, such as coalitional killing, between chimpanzees and humans, arguing that these behavioral tendencies must have existed in the common parent species, and would therefore have been present in prehistoric *Homo sapiens*.

From their book, *Demonic Males: Apes and the Origins of Human Violence*:

> "Chimpanzee-like violence preceded and paved the way
> for human war, making modern humans the dazed
> survivors of a continuous, five-million-year habit of
> lethal aggression."

---

[45] Wrangham has made a very different but very strong contribution to the portrait of early humans in *Catching Fire*, where he presents the argument that the cooking of meat stimulated a cycle of rapid evolution of the human brain. The idea is that the discovery of fire and the fact that cooked meat is far easier to chew and digest made it easier to consume greater amounts of it, greatly boosting the percentage of protein in the paleolithic diet; the energy cost of digestion dropped significantly, and available building blocks for increased tissue density, as well as energy supply to support a larger brain, were abundant. Wrangham's idea has been well-received in academia.

Wrangham has company. David Livingston Smith, in his book *The Most Dangerous Animal: Human Nature and the Origins of War*, focuses not so much on the prehistoric past but on the atrocities of the present, arguing that humans are innately violent, even more so than chimpanzees:

> "Like it or not, war is distinctly human. Apart from the
> raiding behavior of chimpanzees and the so-called wars
> prosecuted by certain species of ants, there is nothing in
> nature that comes anywhere near approximating it."

Smith goes further than Wrangham, arguing that it is likewise part of human nature to demote others of our kind, in order to make them easier to exploit or eliminate:

> "Dehumanization isn't a way of talking. It's a way of
> thinking – a way of thinking that, sadly, comes all too
> easily to us. Dehumanization is a scourge, and has been
> so for millennia. It acts as a psychological lubricant,
> dissolving our inhibitions and inflaming our destructive
> passions. As such, it empowers us to perform acts
> that would, under other circumstances, be unthinkable."

But it is Steven Pinker who leads the charge on claims of inherent human violence. His 2011 book *The Better Angels of Our Nature: Why Violence Has Declined*, he presents a net-hopeful argument that a charting of human rates of homicide and other violent acts per capita will demonstrate that we started out very violent in the prehistoric past and have steadily become less so:

> "If the past is a foreign country, it is a shockingly violent
> one. It is easy to forget how dangerous life used to be,
> how deeply brutality was once woven into the fabric
> of daily existence. Cultural memory pacifies the past,
> leaving us with pale souvenirs whose bloody origins
> have been bleached away."

Part of Pinker's thesis is that genes make us inherently violent, but they can also be their own remedy:

> "Behavioral genetics confirms that aggressive tendencies
> can be inherited, and that gives natural selection material
> to work with in shifting the average violent tendencies of
> a population."

There is certainly much evidence to support the thesis of inherent human violence, and much observational and archaeological evidence confirming the violence of males in particular. Pinker's point about behavioral genetics is an important one, and even more important is that it cuts both ways: It allows us to focus on the question of whether violent behaviors, indisputably present to some degree at all points in the history and prehistory of *Homo sapiens*, were the exception or the rule – a key question in determining how we might proceed toward a *Trek* future.

Can We Ever Boldly Go?

"Human beings are not wicked by nature. We have enough intelligence, goodwill, generosity, and enterprise to turn Earth into a paradise both for ourselves and for the biosphere that gave us birth. We can plausibly accomplish that goal, at least be well on the way, by the end of the present century."

~Edward O. Wilson

American biologist/naturalist Edward O. Wilson's manifesto is more than just optimism; it is his conviction that we *must* make a paradise of Earth, because we're stuck here, even if we someday develop warp drive. He reasons that we simply have no alternative, because we cannot live on other worlds.

Such a proclamation is anathema to any *Trek* fan; we all want to believe, as Gene Roddenberry and Carl Sagan and Arthur C. Clarke did, that life is abundant throughout the universe, even if it doesn't take the form of Vulcans or Andorians or Romulans. Any suggestion to the contrary will inspire a pretty fierce response.

Wilson backs into his thesis from the other side: that all species are inexorably bound to their birthworlds is the reason why Earth has not been visited by intelligent beings from elsewhere.

"All E.T.s have a fatal weakness," he writes in his 2015 book, *The Meaning of Human Existence*. "Their bodies would almost certainly carry microbiomes, entire ecosystems of symbiotic microorganisms comparable to the ones that our own bodies require for day-to-day existence. The E.T. colonists would also be forced to bring crop plants, algae-equivalents, or some other energy-gathering organisms, or at the very least synthetic organisms to provide their food. They would correctly assume that every native species of animal, plant, fungus, and microorganism on Earth is potentially deadly to them and to their symbionts. The reason is that the two living worlds, ours and theirs, are radically different in origin, molecular machinery, and the endless pathways of evolution that produced the life-forms then brought together by colonization. The ecosystems and species of the alien world would be wholly incompatible with our own."

The outcome of such a visitation "would be a biological train wreck," he continues. "The first to perish would be the alien colonists. The residents – us and all of Earth's fauna and flora, to which we are so exquisitely well-adapted – would be unaffected except briefly and very locally. The clash of worlds would not be the same as the ongoing exchange of species of plants and animals between Australia and Africa, or between North and South America. It's true that considerable damage to native ecosystems has recently occurred due to such intercontinental mixing, caused by our own species. Many of the colonists hang on as invasive species, especially in habitats disturbed by humans. A few manage to crowd native species to extinction. But it is nothing like the vicious biological incompatibility that would doom interplanetary colonists. In order to colonize a habitable planet, the aliens would first have to destroy all life on it, down to the last microbe.

"Better to stay at home," he concludes, "for a few more billion years, anyway."

Wilson allows that if there is intelligent life out there somewhere, and if it is capable of interstellar travel, then Nomad-like visitation by robots for the purpose of gathering information about us is at least a distant possibility.

A *Trek* fan will respond to Wilson's thesis with a reply such as this:

The biological incompatibilities between ourselves and the life in otherworldly biospheres may indeed be a challenge, but we can meet that challenge with technology, adapting ourselves and our microbiomes to the new environment – to which Wilson would reply, The divergent paths of biological evolution are all but infinite, and there is no way to know which of those paths any particular planet might have taken, in advance of going there, and thus no way of knowing what technology would need to be developed in advance of going there, and no way of testing that technology in advance.

The *Trek* fan might also say, well, then, if we can't adapt ourselves to the new biosphere, we would still have a Goldilocks planet with water and a breathable atmosphere – maybe we go all Genesis Torpedo on the planet and wipe it clean, then build a human-friend biosphere from scratch? We don't need Wilson's reply to that one; Carol Marcus herself would say, "There can't be so much as a microbe, or the show's off!" Destroying even very primitive life shuts down evolution on such a planet, and that's antithetical to our moral values.

It's fun to think about other worlds, and to dream of seeking them out. But Wilson's toxicity issue demands a serious response, and it must be a well-reasoned, science-based response. Whether such a case can be made or not, his underlying point is one any *Trek* enthusiast will embrace: before we can even seriously consider going to other worlds, we need to learn to take proper care of this one.

As a point of interest, note that two of the people quoted in this book wind up on *both* sides of Roddenberry's vision.

Robert Ardrey promoted the idea that early humans were vicious and violent, and that we are inherently so, while also advocating for group selection as an evolutionary force.

E.O. Wilson has pushed hard the idea that human beings are naturally altruistic, while also warning that we are forever bound to the Earth, and will never go to the stars.

Appendix II: The Great Bird Speaks

"We must question the story logic of having an all-knowing all-powerful God, who creates faulty Humans, and then blames them for his own mistakes."

"If man is to survive, he will have learned to take a delight in the essential differences between men and between cultures. He will learn that differences in ideas and attitudes are a delight, part of life's exciting variety, not something to fear."

"A man either lives life as it happens to him, meets it head-on and licks it, or he turns his back on it and starts to wither away."

"It is the struggle itself that is most important. We must strive to be more than we are. It does not matter that we will not reach our ultimate goal. The effort itself yields its own reward."

"Reality is incredibly larger, infinitely more exciting, than the flesh and blood vehicle we travel in here. If you read science fiction, the more you read it the more you realize that you and the universe are part of the same thing. Science knows still practically nothing about the real nature of matter, energy, dimension, or time; and even less about those remarkable things called life and thought. But whatever the meaning and purpose of this universe, you are a legitimate part of it. And since you are part of the all that is, part of its purpose, there is more to you than just this brief speck of existence. You are just a visitor here in this time and this place, a traveler through it."

"Can all this just be an accident? Or could there be some alien intelligence behind it?"

"*Star Trek* speaks to some basic human needs: that there is a tomorrow—it's not all going to be over with a big flash and a bomb; that the human race is improving; that we have things to be proud of as humans."

"For *Star Trek* proves, as faulty as individual episodes could be, is that the much-maligned common man and common woman has an enormous hunger for brotherhood. They are ready for the twenty-third century now, and they are light-years ahead of their petty governments and their visionless leaders."

"Technology would have long ago made privacy impossible, except that this had only made it more precious and desirable--and in the close confines of starship life, respect for another's privacy had become a powerful tradition."

"Earth is the nest, the cradle, and we'll move out of it."

"The human race is a remarkable creature, one with great potential, and I hope that *Star Trek* has helped to show us what we can be if we believe in ourselves and our abilities."

"It is important to the typical *Star Trek* fan that there is a tomorrow. They pretty much share the 'Star Trek' philosophies about life: the fact that it is wrong to interfere in the evolvement of other peoples, that to be different is not necessarily to be wrong or ugly."

"*Star Trek* says that it has not all happened, it has not all been discovered, that tomorrow can be as challenging and adventurous as any time man has ever lived."

"To be different is not necessarily to be ugly; to have a different idea is not necessarily to be wrong. The worst possible thing is for all of us to begin to look and talk and act and think alike."

"In the 24th century there will be no hunger, there will be no greed, and all the children will know how to read."

"I believe in humanity. We are an incredible species. We're still just a child creature; we're still being nasty to each other. And all children go through those phases. We're growing up, we're moving into adolescence now. When we grow up - man, we're going to be something!"

"*Star Trek* says that it has not all happened, it has not all been discovered, that tomorrow can be as challenging and adventurous as any time man has ever lived."

"I condemn false prophets, I condemn the effort to take away the power of rational decision, to drain people of their free will - and a hell of a lot of money in the bargain. Religions vary in their degree of idiocy, but I reject them all. For most people, religion is nothing more than a substitute for a malfunctioning brain."

"Why are we now going into space? Well, why did we trouble to look past the next mountain? Our prime obligation to ourselves is to make the unknown known. We are on a journey to keep an appointment with whatever we are."

"We stress humanity, and this is done at considerable cost. We can't have a lot of dramatics that other shows get away with - promiscuity, greed, jealousy. None of those have a place in *Star Trek*."

"In a better world, I can do anything. I'll be there in a better world. In a better world, they will not laugh at me or look down their nose at me."

"Almost all of this comes out of my feeling that the human future is bright. We're just beginning. We have wonders ahead of us. I don't see how it can be any other way, with the way the future is going. We now have got a telescope up there. We're photographing the universe. We're inventing the next life form, which is the computer. We're in the midst of it. And it will happen."

"This is a marvelous stew, the human condition. It used to be, the stew was made up of tasteless things back in the feudal days. Now, it's laid over with wonderful things in addition to the bad things. You can't study evolution, particularly the evolution of humanity, that you don't see that it's getting better and better."

"The question of consciousness has always intrigued me. It starts with the question, 'Are we our bodies or are we our consciousness? What are we made up of?'"

"Perhaps one of the primary features of *Star Trek* that made it different from other shows was, it believed that humans are improving - they will vastly improve in the 23rd century."

"There is a tomorrow - we humans are going to make it - we're something. To any young-minded person, that's a very important statement."

"I have nothing but admiration for this silly race of ours. Even with the Hitlers in it and so on. Sometimes it goes into ugliness, but in all though, it is a beauty. It's like a rose, which also has thorns. We're something."

"We're capable of great things. And I've no doubt that the creature that follows us will be capable of even more. Evolution didn't stop with us: 'Oh great and beautiful mankind! We've made it!' -- We haven't. [Evolution] can go on forever."

Gene Roddenberry

1921-1991

Appendix III: Other Voices

"As brainy social animals, human beings evolved to be consummate actors whose survival and ability to reproduce depend on the quality of our performances. We enter the world prepared to perform roles and manage the impressions of others, with the ultimate evolutionary aim of getting along and getting ahead in the social groups that define who we are."
~Dan P. McAdams

"Our way of thinking – both individually and collectively – is dominated by short-term horizons and distorted by habits of thought inherited from our prehistoric ancestors, who had to survive threats very different from the ones we face today."
~Al Gore, *The Future*

"The problem holding everything up thus far is that *Homo sapiens* is an innately dysfunctional species. We are hampered by the Paleolithic Curse: genetic adaptations that worked very well for millions of years of hunter-gatherer existence but are increasingly a hindrance in a globally urban and technoscientific society. We seem unable to stabilize either economic policies or the means of governance higher than the level of a village. Further, the great majority of people worldwide remain in the thrall of tribal organized religions, led by men who claim supernatural power in order to compete for the obedience and resources of the faithful. We are addicted to tribal conflict, which is harmless and entertaining if sublimated into team sports, but deadly when expressed as real-world ethnic, religious, and ideological struggles."
~Edward O. Wilson

"Breath is to life as play is to intelligence."
~Randy McChesney

"I like the dreams of the future better than the history of the past."
~Thomas Jefferson

"The image of humanity, warped by bloodlust, inevitably marching off to kill, is a powerful myth and an important prop of militarism in our society. Despite its lack of scientific credibility, there will remain those 'hard-headed realists' who continue to believe in it, congratulating themselves for their 'courage to face the truth,' resolutely oblivious to the myth behind their 'reality.'"

~R. Brian Ferguson

"No tribe could hold together if murder, robbery, treachery, etc. were common; consequently such crimes within the limits of the same tribe 'are branded with everlasting infamy'; but excite no such sentiments beyond these limits."
~Charles Darwin

"Humans have evolved levels of cooperation that are unprecedented among primate species. You can see it even in babies. Say you are playing with a baby and begin to put the toys in a box. If you point to one of the toys, the baby is likely to put it in the box (Liebal et al. 2009)... Human babies are more likely than other primates to follow another's pointing or gaze. Thus, even before adults have socialized them, babies show tendencies to be in sync with the social behavior of others, to infer others' intentions to cooperate, and to prefer cooperation in others."
~Anthony Biglan, *The Nurture Effect: How the Science of Human Behavior Can Improve Our Lives and Our World*

"A day may come when these recovered memories may grow as vivid as if we in our own persons had been there and shared the thrill and the fear of those primordial days; a day may come when the great beasts of the past will leap to life again in our imaginations, when we shall walk again in vanished scenes, stretch painted limbs we thought were dust, and feel again the sunshine of a million years ago."
~H.G. Welles, *The Grisly Folk*

"Violence is the last refuge of the incompetent."
~Isaac Asimov

"A human being should be able to change a diaper, plan an invasion, butcher a hog, conn a ship, design a building, write a sonnet, balance accounts, build a wall, set a bone, comfort the dying, take orders, give orders, cooperate, act alone, solve equations, analyze a new problem, program a computer, cook a tasty meal, fight efficiently, die gallantly. Specialization is for insects!"
~Robert Heinlein

"When kids look up to great scientists the way they do to great musicians and actors, civilization will jump to the next level."
~Brian Greene

"Back in the sixties when *Star Trek* debuted, you couldn't help but notice that the bridge of the Starship *Enterprise* was a multi-cultural, multi-national, multi-intelligent species sort of arrangement. It portrayed, to my impressionable young mind, an inevitable kumbaya, pluralistic future. It's only lately that I've come to understand how naive that world view was. I now see that human nature, particularly during times of stress, becomes tribalistic, not pluralistic. Which is neither good nor bad. It's probably just how we're wired, a survival mechanism baked into our DNA. Under pressure, the prime directive is to protect the tribe. Genetically, that makes perfect sense. Human beings without a tribe tend to starve or get eaten. Now I don't want to cast aspersions, or "throw shade" as the kids like to say, but I would like to point out one thing I find painfully obvious: He's not in your tribe. He's not in my tribe. In fact, if you look closely, you'll see he belongs to no tribe. And he never really has. Make of that what you will."
~Chuck Lorre, #575

"Agriculture was one of the great stupid mistakes in human history. That was a bad move! The main advantage of agriculture is that is allows you to concentrate capital and resources in the hands of a few people and start making stratified societies and all sorts of nasty stuff..."
~Prof. Robert Sapolsky

"They used to say if man could fly, he'd have wings, but he did fly. He discovered he had to. Do you wish that the first Apollo mission hadn't reached the moon, or that we hadn't gone on to Mars and then to the nearest star? That's like saying you wish that you still operated with scalpels and sewed your patients up with catgut like your great-great-great-great grandfather used to. I'm in command. I could order this, but I'm not - because Doctor McCoy is right in pointing out the enormous danger potential in any contact with life and intelligence as fantastically advanced as this, but I must point out that the possibilities – the potential for knowledge and advancement – is equally great. Risk! Risk is our business. That's what this starship is all about. That's why we're aboard her!"
~Capt. James T. Kirk's 'Risk is Our Business' speech

"Our posturings, our imagined self-importance, the delusion that we have some privileged position in the Universe, are challenged by this point of pale light. Our planet is a lonely speck in the great enveloping cosmic dark. In our obscurity, in all this vastness, there is no hint that help will come from elsewhere to save us from ourselves."
~Carl Sagan, *Pale Blue Dot:*
A Vision of the Human Future in Space

"People went and looked at [present-day hunter gatherers] closely (anthropologists in the Sixties) and discovered these people were not starving; these people were having a very comfortable existence in lots of ways. If you're going to be in the developing world, you would much rather be a hunter-gatherer than an agriculturalist or a nomadic pastoralist; you have a much better diet, far more variety, far more resistance to famine, because you're eating three hundred different plant species instead of the six or seven things you're cultivating; you have far less work – agriculturalists work like maniacs, these hunter-gatherers work three, four hours a day for their calories and spend the rest of their time doing social anthropology or whatever they do there; it's a much easier lifestyle."
~Robert Sapolsky

"The Earth is a very small stage in a vast cosmic arena. Think of the endless cruelties visited by the inhabitants of one corner of this pixel on the scarcely distinguishable inhabitants of some other corner, how frequent their misunderstandings, how eager they are to kill one another, how fervent their hatreds. Think of the rivers of blood spilled by all those generals and emperors so that, in glory and triumph, they could become the momentary masters of a fraction of a dot."
~Carl Sagan, *Pale Blue Dot: A Vision of the Human Future in Space*

"So the universe is not quite as you thought it was? You'd better rearrange your beliefs, then. Because you certainly can't rearrange the universe."
~Isaac Asimov

"Modern man has been alienated from himself, from his fellow men, and from nature. He has been transformed into a commodity, experiences his life forces as an investment which must bring him the maximum profit obtainable under existing market conditions. Human relations are essentially those of alienated automatons, each basing his security on staying close to the herd, and not being different in thought, feeling, or action. While everybody tries to be as close as possible to the rest, everybody remains utterly alone, pervaded by the deep sense of insecurity, anxiety and guilt which always results when human separateness cannot be overcome."
~Erich Fromm, *The Art of Loving*

"It is chauvinistic to treat humans as though they were the end point of evolution. They are only one of millions of end products – one tiny twig."
~Richard Dawkins

"There is no finer investment for any community than putting milk into babies."
~Winston Churchill

"Look again at that dot. That's here. That's home. That's us. On it everyone you love, everyone you know, everyone you ever heard of, every human being who ever was, lived out their lives. The aggregate of our joy and suffering, thousands of confident religions, ideologies, and economic doctrines, every hunter and forager, every hero and coward, every creator and destroyer of civilization, every king and peasant, every young couple in love, every mother and father, hopeful child, inventor and explorer, every teacher of morals, every corrupt politician, every 'superstar,' every 'supreme leader,' every saint and sinner in the history of our species lived there - on a mote of dust suspended in a sunbeam."

~Carl Sagan, *Pale Blue Dot:
A Vision of the Human Future in Space*

"As man advances in civilization, and small tribes are united into larger communities, the simplest reason would tell each individual that he ought to extend his social instincts and sympathies to all the members of the same nation, though personally unknown to him. This point being once reached, there is only an artificial barrier to prevent his sympathies extending to the men of all nations and races."

~Charles Darwin

"Hunter-gatherers practiced the most successful and longest-lasting life style in human history. In contrast, we're still struggling with the mess into which agriculture has tumbled us, and it's unclear whether we can solve it. Suppose that an archaeologist who had visited from outer space were trying to explain human history to his fellow spacelings. He might illustrate the results of his digs by a 24-hour clock on which one hour represents 100,000 years of real past time. If the history of the human race began at midnight, then we would now be almost at the end of our first day. We lived as hunter-gatherers for nearly the whole of that day, from midnight through dawn, noon, and sunset. Finally, at 11:54 p.m. we adopted agriculture. As our second midnight approaches, will the plight of famine-stricken peasants gradually spread to engulf us all? Or will we somehow achieve those seductive blessings that we imagine behind agriculture's glittering facade, and that have so far eluded us?"
~Jared Diamond

"Most people think there are a lot of bad people running around in the world. There aren't a lot of bad people, there are a lot of bad ideas, and bad ideas are worse than bad people because bad ideas are contagious – bad ideas get good people to do horrible things."
~Sam Harris

"The beginning of modern science can be dated from the time when such general questions as, 'How was the universe created? What is matter made of? What is the essence of life?' were replaced by such limited questions as 'How does a stone fall? How does water flow in a tube? How does blood circulate in vessels?' This substitution had an amazing result. While asking general questions led to limited answers, asking limited questions turned out to provide more and more general answers."
~ Francois Jacob

"We are the miracle of force and matter, making itself over into imagination and will," he said. "Incredible! The Life Force experimenting with forms. You for one. Me for another. The Universe has shouted itself alive, and we are one of the shouts."
~Ray Bradbury

"You know the greatest danger facing us is ourselves, an irrational fear of the unknown. But there's no such thing as the unknown — only things temporarily hidden, temporarily not understood."
~Capt. James T. Kirk's
'No Such Thing as the Unknown' speech

"Once we have computer outlets in every home, each of them hooked up to enormous libraries, where you can ask any question and be given answers, you can look up something you're interested in knowing, however silly it might seem to someone else."
~Isaac Asimov in 1988

"The big difference when [a child today] grows up — in fact you won't have to wait for the year 2001 — is that he will have in his own house ... a console through which he can talk to his friendly local computer and get all the information he needs for his everyday life, like his bank statements, theatre reservations—all the information you need in the course of living in a complex modern society. This will be in a compact form in his own house. You'll have a television screen...and a keyboard and he'll talk to the computer and get information from it. And he'll take it as much for granted as we take the telephone."
~Arthur C. Clarke, 1974

"Human nature is complex. Even if we do have inclinations toward violence, we also have inclination to empathy, to cooperation, to self-control."
~Steven Pinker

"Universal peace as a result of cumulative effort through centuries past might come into existence quickly—not unlike a crystal that suddenly forms in a solution which has been slowly prepared."
~Nikola Tesla

"Humans aren't as good as we should be in our capacity to empathize with feelings and thoughts of others, be they humans or other animals on Earth. So maybe part of our formal education should be training in empathy. Imagine how different the world would be if, in fact, that were 'reading, writing, arithmetic, empathy.'
~Neil deGrasse Tyson

"A prerequisite to empathy is simply paying attention to the person in pain."
~Daniel Goleman

"Positive social emotions like compassion and empathy are generally good for us, and we want to encourage them. But do we know how to most reliably raise children to care about the suffering of other people? I'm not sure we do."
~Sam Harris

"Human decency is not derived from religion.
It precedes it."
~Christopher Hitchens

"We all do better when we work together. Our differences
do matter, but our common humanity matters more."
~Bill Clinton

"We have been to the moon, we have charted the depths
of the ocean and the heart of the atom, but we have a
fear of looking inward to ourselves because we sense that
is where all the contradictions flow together."
~Terence McKenna

"It has been said that astronomy is a humbling and
character-building experience. There is perhaps no better
demonstration of the folly of human conceits than this
distant image of our tiny world. To me, it underscores our
responsibility to deal more kindly with one another, and
to preserve and cherish the pale blue dot, the only home
we've ever known."
~Carl Sagan, *Pale Blue Dot:*
A Vision of the Human Future in Space

"Strange is our situation here upon earth. Each of us comes for a short visit, not knowing why, yet sometimes seeming to a divine purpose. From the standpoint of daily life, however, there is one thing we do know: That we are here for the sake of other men —above all for those upon whose smile and well-being our own happiness depends, for the countless unknown souls with whose fate we are connected by a bond of sympathy. Many times a day, I realize how much my outer and inner life is built upon the labors of people, both living and dead, and how earnestly I must exert myself in order to give in return as much as I have received and am still receiving."
~Albert Einstein

"If you want to make peace with your enemy, you have to work with your enemy. Then he becomes your partner."
~Nelson Mandela

"Competition has been shown to be useful up to a certain point and no further, but cooperation, which is the thing we must strive for today, begins where competition leaves off."
~Franklin D. Roosevelt

"Being a Humanist means trying to behave decently without expectation of rewards or punishment after you are dead."
~Kurt Vonnegut, Jr.

"How can a three-pound mass of jelly that you can hold in your palm imagine angels, contemplate the meaning of infinity, and even question its own place in the cosmos? Especially awe inspiring is the fact that any single brain, including yours, is made up of atoms that were forged in the hearts of countless, far-flung stars billions of years ago. These particles drifted for eons and light-years until gravity and change brought them together here, now. These atoms now form a conglomerate- your brain- that can not only ponder the very stars that gave it birth but can also think about its own ability to think and wonder about its own ability to wonder. With the arrival of humans, it has been said, the universe has suddenly become conscious of itself. This, truly, it the greatest mystery of all."
~V.S. Ramachandran

"Selfish members win within groups, but groups of altruists best groups of selfish members."
~Edward O. Wilson

"We're human beings with the blood of a million savage years on our hands! But we can stop it. We can admit that we're killers . . . but we're not going to kill today. That's all it takes! Knowing that we're not going to kill — today!"
~Capt. James T. Kirk's 'We're Not Going to Kill Today' speech

"Nothing truly valuable can be achieved except by the unselfish cooperation of many individuals."
~Albert Einstein

"I decline to accept the end of man. It is easy enough to say that man is immortal because he will endure: that when the last ding-dong of doom has clanged and faded from the last worthless rock hanging tideless in the last red and dying evening, that even then there will still be one more sound: that of his puny inexhaustible voice, still talking. I refuse to accept this. I believe that man will not merely endure: he will prevail. He is immortal, not because he alone among creatures has an inexhaustible voice, but because he has a soul, a spirit capable of compassion and sacrifice and endurance."
~William Faulkner

"After all, what else did we have going for us? Nothing, except we ran like crazy and stuck together. Humans are among the most communal and cooperative of all primates; our sole defense in a fang-filled world was our solidarity, and there's no reason to think we suddenly disbanded our most crucial challenge, the hunt for food. I remembered what the Seri Indians told Scott Carrier after the sun had set on their persistence-hunting days.

'It was better before,' a Seri elder lamented. 'We did everything as a family. The whole community was a family. We shared everything and cooperated, but now there is a lot of arguing and bickering, every man for himself.

'Running didn't just make the Seris a people...it also made them better people.'"

~Christopher McDougall

"I sometimes try to imagine what would have happened if we'd known the bonobo first and the chimpanzee only later - or not at all. The discussion about human evolution might not revolve as much around violence, warfare and male dominance, but rather around sexuality, empathy, caring and cooperation. What a different intellectual landscape we would occupy!"

~Frans de Waal

"I do not fear computers. I fear the lack of them."
~Isaac Asimov

"Our greatest fear should not be of failure, but of succeeding at things that don't really matter."
~Dwight L. Moody

"To call woman the weaker sex is a libel; it is man's injustice to woman. If by strength is meant brute strength, then, indeed, is woman less brute than man. If by strength is meant moral power, then woman is immeasurably man's superior. Has she not greater intuition, is she not more self-sacrificing, has she not greater powers of endurance, has she not greater courage? Without her, man could not be. If nonviolence is the law of our being, the future is with woman. Who can make a more effective appeal to the heart than woman?"
~Mahatma Gandhi, *To the Women of India*
(*Young India*, Oct. 4, 1930)"

"One of the sanest, surest, and most generous joys of life comes from being happy over the good fortune of others."
~Robert A. Heinlein

"Certainly studying human evolution makes you think about the future. It makes you realize how much baggage we carry forward with us at all times - how we are, in a sense, fish out of water nowadays. We're living in an environmental context that's radically different than the one in which we evolved."
~Terrence Deacon

"Let us make our future now, and let us make our dreams tomorrow's reality."
~Malala Yousafzai

"The Earth is the only world known so far to harbor life. There is nowhere else, at least in the near future, to which our species could migrate. Visit, yes. Settle, not yet. Like it or not, for the moment the Earth is where we make our stand."
~Carl Sagan, *Pale Blue Dot:*
A Vision of the Human Future in Space

"If knowledge can create problems, it is not through ignorance that we can solve them."
~Isaac Asimov

"In neo-classical economic theory, it is claimed without evidence that people are basically self-seeking, that they want above all the satisfaction of their material desires: what economists call 'maximising utility'. The ultimate objective of mankind is economic growth, and that is maximized only through raw, and lightly regulated, competition. If the rewards of this system are spread unevenly, that is a necessary price. Others on the planet are to be regarded as either customers, competitors or factors of production. Effects upon the planet itself are mere 'externalities' to the model, with no reckoning of the cost - at least for now. Nowhere in this analysis appears factors such as human cooperation, love, trust, compassion or hatred, curiosity or beauty. Nowhere appears the concept of meaning. What cannot be measured is ignored. But the trouble is that once our basic needs for shelter and food have been met, these factors may be the most important of all."

~Carne Ross

"If you get up in the morning and think the future is going to be better, it is a bright day. Otherwise, it's not."
~Elon Musk

"When men yield up the privilege of thinking, the last shadow of liberty quits the horizon."

~Thomas Paine

"It is not the critic who counts; not the man who points out how the strong man stumbles, or where the doer of deeds could have done them better. The credit belongs to the man who is actually in the arena, whose face is marred by dust and sweat and blood; who strives valiantly; who errs, who comes short again and again, because there is no effort without error and shortcoming; but who does actually strive to do the deeds; who knows great enthusiasms, the great devotions; who spends himself in a worthy cause; who at the best knows in the end the triumph of high achievement, and who at the worst, if he fails, at least fails while daring greatly, so that his place shall never be with those cold and timid souls who neither know victory nor defeat."
~Theodore Roosevelt

"Never let your sense of morals get in the way of doing what's right."
~Isaac Asimov

"Freedom can exist only in the society of knowledge. Without learning, men are incapable of knowing their rights, and where learning is confined to a few people, liberty can be neither equal nor universal."
~Benjamin Rush

"I have a foreboding of an America in my children's or grandchildren's time – when the United States is a service and information economy; when nearly all the key manufacturing industries have slipped away to other countries; when awesome technological power are in the hands of a very few, and no one representing the public interest can even grasp the issues; when the people have lost the ability to set their own agendas or knowledgeably question those in authority; when, clutching our crystals and nervously consulting our horoscopes, our critical faculties in decline, unable to distinguish between what feels good and what's true, we slide, almost without noticing, back into superstition and darkness."

~Carl Sagan

"Two possibilities exist: either we are alone in the Universe or we are not. Both are equally terrifying."
~Arthur C. Clarke

"I am made from the dust of the stars, and the ocean flows in my veins..."
~Neil Peart, Rush

From

The Trek Equation

Class-M Planets and the Evolution of Intelligent Humanoid Life

Entropy, Interrupted

Revisiting the work of physicist Jeremy England, we're reminded that his new theory posits that the conflict between entropy (the idea that the universe tears down order to create chaos) and life (the continuous build-up of ever more complicated organic molecules and increasingly complex living organisms) is solved by a simple principle: it is the nature of matter to *spread energy*.

At the most extreme macro level, this makes perfect sense and is observably happening: since the Big Bang, energy has been pouring out into the universe like spilled water on a kitchen floor, finding every possible path to every possible destination. Like kitchen furniture, the specks of matter in the universe - planets, comets, asteroids, interstellar dust - block and deflect that energy. And, as kitchen furniture gets wet, matter in the path of energy soaks it up.

Per Einstein, we know that matter itself - including us! - is simply condensed energy. That condensation is nothing more than an incidental consequence of certain thermodynamic conditions in certain places in space. Our planet, its atmosphere, its water, all the life on it - including us! - are an incidental mass of condensed energy, no different than all the other chunks of not-quite-energy dancing around stars and wandering through cold interstellar space.

Except...

Here on this particular planet, things are a little bit different.

Spreading Energy

First, a bit more of England: his team observes in their published papers that the Spread Energy imperative, elegant and simple, is observable everywhere in Nature. So ubiquitous is it, when sought out, that it is clearly the rule, not the exception: the properties of matter, both living and non-, all give service to this imperative. The Spread Energy imperative appears to be the very nature of Nature (though the theory is not yet proven).

England appears as a character in Dan Brown's novel *Origin*, which provides examples of natural organization that promotes entropy: simple objects, like snowflakes - frozen water - which spontaneously form complex shapes to most efficiently distribute light and heat. They cannot *not* do so. Quartz displays similar properties – elegant organization of non-living matter, optimized to radiate energy efficiently.

Origin's examples include weather, which can be characterized as complex systems that optimize to dissipate energy in the atmosphere, from the pressure-relieving vortex of a tornado to the electrical discharge of a lightning bolt, dispelling the structured ganging of charged particles in a thundercloud.

Even the simple mechanisms of life demonstrate England's principle – and life turns out to be matter's best innovation yet, when it comes to the spreading of energy. Photosynthesis, *Origin* points out, is a marvelous example: a tree absorbs a steady stream of sunlight, absconding with some of it to extend and replicate itself, while dissipating the remainder as infrared radiation: increased entropy.

And as for DNA, the engine of organic replication – it, too, exists in the service of entropy: a forest, for instance, can dissipate far more energy than a single tree.

If all of this is how Nature really works - and it appears increasingly likely - then England's Spread Energy principle explains how organic molecules came to be, and why increasing complexity is their rule: what we call life is in fact just another expression of matter's inherent imperative to get out of energy's way, and to exploit energy in that endeavor.

(This new feature of the universe, by the way, closes the final gap that God has been filling since Darwin. With the tendency of organic molecules to form under certain thermodynamic conditions, and for those molecules to form increasingly complex structures, the origin of life is now explained in full - the need for a 'Creator' has finally expired. The question, "How do living systems arise from non-living matter?" has finally been answered, if England is correct. This is a major theme of *Origin*.)

Physicists have already skipped ahead to the end of the universe's book: in the last pages of the final chapter, it will experience 'heat death' - the final cessation of all energy exchange, as there will eventually be no remaining thermodynamic fuel for entropic processes. England's model not only supports this long-accepted conclusion - it helps explain it.

Between now and the death of the universe, per England, the energy that it contains will continue to spread relentlessly - and all the specks of condensation, all the matter, will inadvertently interrupt that spread, catching and trapping energy in the process. And that captured energy will cause the substance of that matter, the cold particles that cause it to be, to rally for its release, scrambling to combine with other particles in whatever way will promote the energy.

There is no other outcome. All of physics, all of reality, all the laws of Nature yet discovered, bow in service to this unceasing agenda.

...including, again, us.

The Last Resort

It is matter's job to get out of energy's way, however it can, as fast as it can. It is energy's job, when it attempts to spread and finds itself thwarted by intervening matter, to infiltrate that matter and do what it must to push through; and, if possible, cause that matter to return to its own natural state – to *become* energy, when conditions are favorable.

If England's inspiration causes us to reconsider the origins and purpose of life, how does that inform our opinions about whether there's any more of it out there in the universe?

If anything, the England Imperative - *Spread Energy!* - makes the universe an easier place to understand. We are already very clear on the laws of thermodynamics, and so the imperative isn't exactly a sharp turn. But it casts a new light on our assumption that since we live in a universe where the elements of life are abundant, given uncounted billions of opportunities to occur, life will certainly make many appearances.

The England Imperative strongly suggests that life is only going to arise in places where matter can't easily spread energy in a less complicated way. Energy, interrupted by matter, will push through the path of least resistance; matter, organizing to optimize energy's quest, will only become as complex as it needs to be to accomplish that mission. Put another way, life – as the most complex of matter's mechanisms for dissipating energy – is a last resort.

A wickedly simple expression of the England Imperative might be an asteroid orbiting a star - composed of pure iron, let's say, and spinning slowly. The area of the asteroid facing the star will absorb energy from the star, then shed it into cold space as it rotates. It is, at most, a very temporary interruption of energy's journey to where. Nothing as intricate as life is necessary for the asteroid to perform its essential energy hand-off.

Even if the asteroid contained the elements of life, it wouldn't matter: because the thermodynamic system of the asteroid is so simple and performs so efficiently, nothing else is needed - and the additional conditions we know to be necessary for life are absent, in any case.

But an amazing thing happens when we begin to add those conditions: we begin to see direct parallels between the conditions required for life and the complexity of the energy capture of the place where it can take root. Put another way, a celestial body of great thermodynamic complexity and a planet that has conditions friendly to the emergence of life are one and the same.

The more thermodynamically complex the planet, the greater its friendliness to the emergence of life.

Using Earth as our only real baseline, we can observe that even with its staggeringly complex thermodynamic systems, life took its sweet time developing here. Once it did, it began doing its job - *spreading energy!* - and it is no great undertaking to chart the changes in the thermodynamics of the Earth in parallel with the increasing complexity of its emerging biosphere. What had to happen for such a system to emerge was for the planet's thermodynamic complexity to occur in the first place.

Let's examine that complexity briefly.

Complexities

The most famous of the characteristics of a life-bearing planet is that it be a Goldilocks planet. This means the planet exists in its parent star's *circumstellar habitable zone* (CHZ) - not too close, not too far away - so that its surface can support liquid water. The not-too-close/not-too-far, then, translates to not-too-hot/not-too-cold, in terms of surface temperature.

To have liquid water on its surface, the planet must have atmospheric pressure to hold it in place - and to retain an atmosphere heavy enough for that kind of pressure, it must be impervious to solar winds, which would ordinarily strip away the atmosphere of a planet so close to its star. Earth passes this test (while, for instance, Mars does not), possessing a rotating liquid nickel-iron core (a natural dynamo) that gives the planet a solar radiation-repelling magnetic field. [Venus possesses only a sparse magnetic field, yet holds an atmosphere far denser than Earth's; even so, the consequences of this are life-prohibitive - the solar winds are indeed eroding its upper atmosphere, and that activity has been depleting the planet of low-mass hydrogen and oxygen ions for billions of years, ridding it of all the water it may have originally possessed.]

A planet must also rotate at a certain pace - fast enough to pass heat in the course of rotation such that the surface water doesn't ever get hot enough to boil outright, but slowly enough that some of it evaporates, in order to carry water to land by way of clouds. And its mass must be such that it creates a gravitational field wherein life, once it forms, is secure without being crushed.

These characteristics, in combination, put a planet in an entirely different thermodynamic class than a simple iron asteroid. As the planet rotates, it will catch and release heat, as the asteroid does - but with liquid water on its surface and a gentle thermal cycle, vast amounts of energy will nonetheless be trapped to endlessly cycle between land, sea, and air.

The endless cycling of energy creates for Earth an England problem: the matter contained within this huge thermal vista must further organize and complexify in the service of spreading it. Snowflakes happen; tornadoes spring up.

But even that isn't enough, thermodynamically, to create a need for an energy-spreading mechanism as complex as life.

The Earth traps energy above and beyond storing it in air and water and rocks: it shakes and stirs it like a bartender.

Earth spins on an axis, as all planets do. But the spin of the Earth literally has a twist: the planet's axis is tilted, rather than perpendicular to the solar plane. This is, of course, the basis of the seasons. And the seasons are, almost by definition, the gradual shifting of energy from one planetary region to another, in yet another endless thermal cycle, as it revolves around the sun.

And the shaking and stirring goes further still: even more thermodynamically important than the Earth's axial tilt, perhaps, is the gravitational effects of its oversized moon. At one-quarter the size of the Earth itself, the moon is by far the largest satellite of a planet known to exist, ratio-wise.

The consequence, of course, is the intense tidal forces it brings: the moon churns the planet's oceans, generating still more energy to be trapped in liquid matter. The Earth's oceans are literally vast reservoirs of energy.

Now the complexity of the Earth has it working overtime to spread energy, because there are so many constantly-interacting systems trapping and re-trapping energy within - and new mechanisms for spreading it must rally to the task. Elements must combine, molecules become more intricate. New systems must interrupt the existing ones, to push against the bulwark of this tense equilibrium.

Now Life emerges. Self-replicating energy couriers of microscopic size, dedicated to scooping up energy from the environment and radiating it out, with far more intensity than a snowflake and far more intricacy than a tornado. A whole new chapter begins, as life interrupts not only the equilibrium of Earth's dancing thermodynamic systems, but their chemical composition as well. Carbon dioxide, methane, and other heat-trapping molecules of the sort that are currently broiling Venus become essential players in this disruption, paradoxically leveraged to solve the problem they themselves create. If Earth was a complicated story before, now it's a James Joyce novel.

And the supreme complexity in the system – *life!* – serves to introduce new complications that perpetuate the precarious balance between thermodynamic systems, even as they succeed in spreading energy to high heaven. We have named those complications *flora* and *fauna*.

In its simplest forms, life is a marvelous dissipative adaptation; even in an incarnation as simple as algae, it absorbs and redistributes energy, using some of it to replicate itself and thereby increase its utility, thus contributing to entropy. And as we've noted above, more sophisticated forms - land-based plant life being a great example - are even more impactful, turning an empty expanse of heat-absorbing dirt into a sprawling, infrared-radiant entropy engine that will spread and spread.

Algae and plants - all forms of life, really – are reorganizations of matter in the service of energy redistribution. But unlike snowflakes and tornadoes and other transitory, one-off mechanisms, living organisms themselves take on the role of energy trap: they collect more energy than their raw materials would, if dissociated, and apply that energy to the purposes of entropy.

And when we get to animal life, the England Imperative gets more creative still: animals don't just absorb solar energy, exploit it, then redistribute it; animals can capture and trap the energy *of other living things*, other energy traps. They extract the energy of other plants and animals. In this process, entropy is served on yet another level: the animal consumption of other forms of life, in releasing that life's energy, breaks it down - *order into chaos* - entropy, once again.

This stupendous innovation is remarkable enough in itself. But it gives rise to one of the most unusual features of the Earth's biosphere: the thermodynamically precarious swap of gases between plant life and animal life. Respiration is experienced by plants and animals alike, with plants emitting oxygen and animals emitting carbon dioxide - a complementary accommodation that benefits both, keeping both kingdoms of life in equilibrium. If either kingdom were to vanish from the Earth, the other would be hard-pressed to survive.

And it grows more complicated still: as animal life has taken the lead as both the premiere redistributor of energy on the planet and its most explicit and dedicated hoarder, it simultaneously (and unwittingly) contributes to the planet's entropy interruption: carbon dioxide and methane, the two gases animals emit, are themselves energy traps. They capture and retain heat; when expelled into the atmosphere, they cause the atmosphere itself to hoard more energy than before.

Repurposed

In hindsight, the emergence of life here on Earth seems inevitable; but the take-home point is that the Earth is as thermodynamically different even from planets of comparable size as an internal combustion engine is from a wind-up watch. We are children of the most unlikely of planets. To say that Earth is one in a billion would be almost certainly understate. And, as a side note, the implications of the England Imperative make the ubiquity of complex life in the universe a *very* distant possibility. It is highly improbable that the universe is teeming with life – which makes the life here on Earth all the more precious. □ □

We can, if England's theory proves true, employ it as a predictive tool as we venture out into the universe: encountering new worlds, we would estimate the likelihood of finding life or something like it based on the world's observable energy traps, its thermodynamic complexity. The more straightforward its energy transfer, the less need for an energy dissipation system as intricate as life.

Here on Earth itself, however, it would have been impossible, given the planet's staggering energy burden, for life□*not*□to have emerged: our planet is a clogged energy sink, capturing the radiation of the sun and hoarding it shamelessly, passing it from system to system, releasing to the night only what it absolutely can't permanently ensnare during the day.

The conclusion is simple and profound and deeply disturbing: we are products of entropy interruption. And our purpose, as far as the universe is concerned, is the spreading of energy. We are here only because in this universe, elements combine in the way that most efficiently pushes energy along, and our particular molecules happen to be situated in the mother of all energy traps.

Any purpose beyond that transcends that of the universe - and is entirely ours to define.

Stars are the forges of energy, emitting it endlessly in an effort to warm the void; planets are interrupters of that entropy; and we are, ironically, planetary disrupters.

We are both agents of and disruptors of entropy. We, the highest form of life, having emerged as reality's champions of energy dissipation, are uniquely positioned to seize the reins of energy distribution – and have already begun doing so, in the order we have created for ourselves out of the raw materials of the Earth. As self-directed entropy engines, we can use our power to increase the interruption of entropy in the service of order, redirecting the dissipation of energy in a manner that complements our industry as the gases of plants and animals complement one another. We can refine our powers of disruption, redirect the role of matter, and leverage entropy's chaos as a means, not an end.

We can, put simply, repurpose the universe.

Origin, indeed...

If you enjoyed
Chasing the Enterprise,
leave a review on Amazon.com!

See more of
the *Boldly Go!* series
on the following pages!

EXPLORING THE ETHICS OF THE FINAL FRONTIER

STAR TREK AND HUMANISM

Living by the Star Trek Ethos in a Troubled World

SCOTT ROBINSON

BOLDLY GOING — BOOK #1

*What would it take to actually build
the world Star Trek imagined?*

CELEBRATING THE HUMANITY OF THE FINAL FRONTIER

TO SUMMON THE FUTURE

CELEBRATING TREK AND HUMAN SOCIAL PROGRESS

SCOTT ROBINSON

BOLDLY GOING — BOOK #3

A TREK GUIDE TO PROGRESSIVE ACTION

RESISTANCE IS *NOT* FUTILE!

A TREK GUIDE TO PROGRESSIVE ACTION

SCOTT ROBINSON

BOLDLY GOING — BOOK #4

12 TREK RULES FOR LIVING

Living the Star Trek Ethos

SCOTT ROBINSON

BOLDLY GOING — BOOK #5

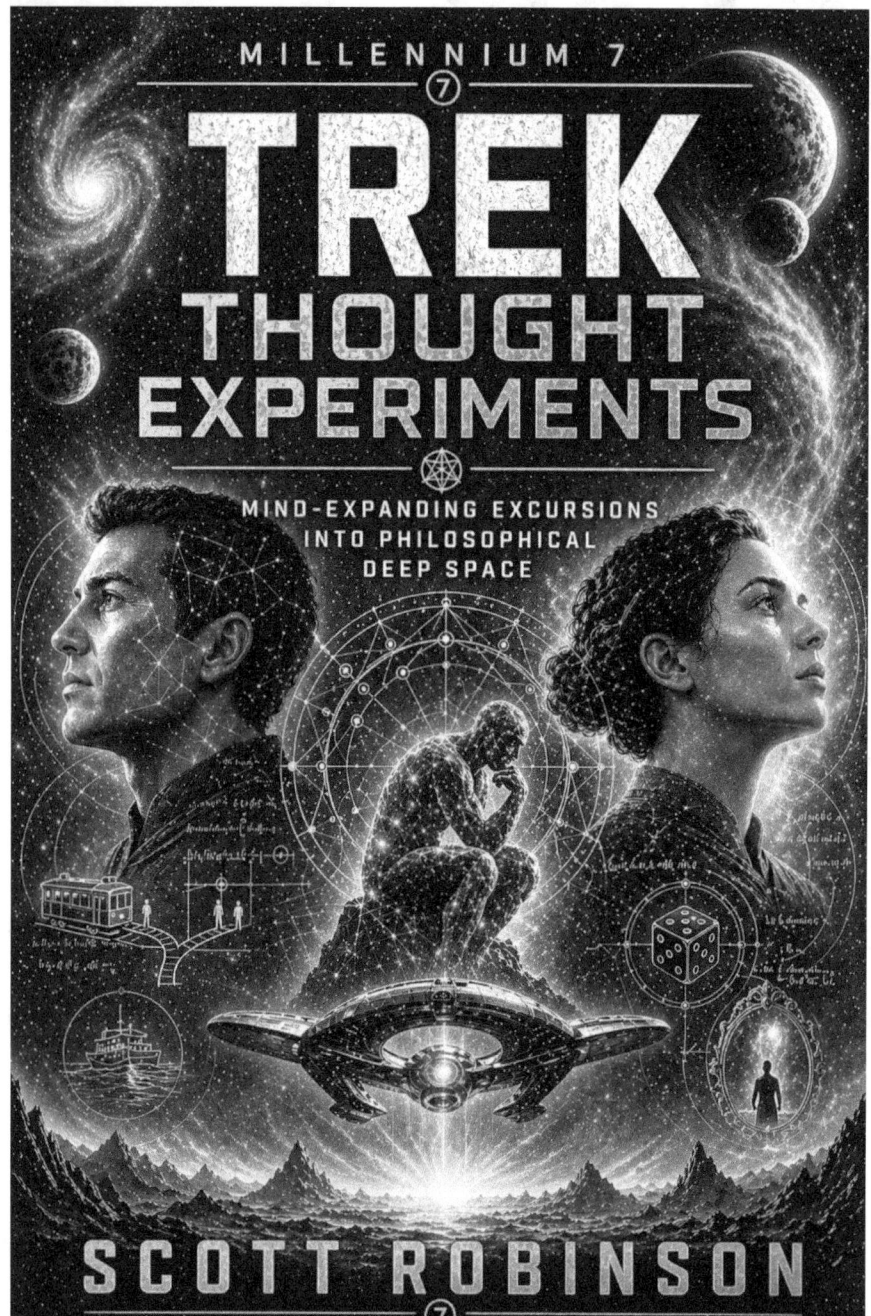

MILLENNIUM 7

⑦

TREK
THOUGHT
EXPERIMENTS

MIND-EXPANDING EXCURSIONS
INTO PHILOSOPHICAL
DEEP SPACE

SCOTT ROBINSON

⑦

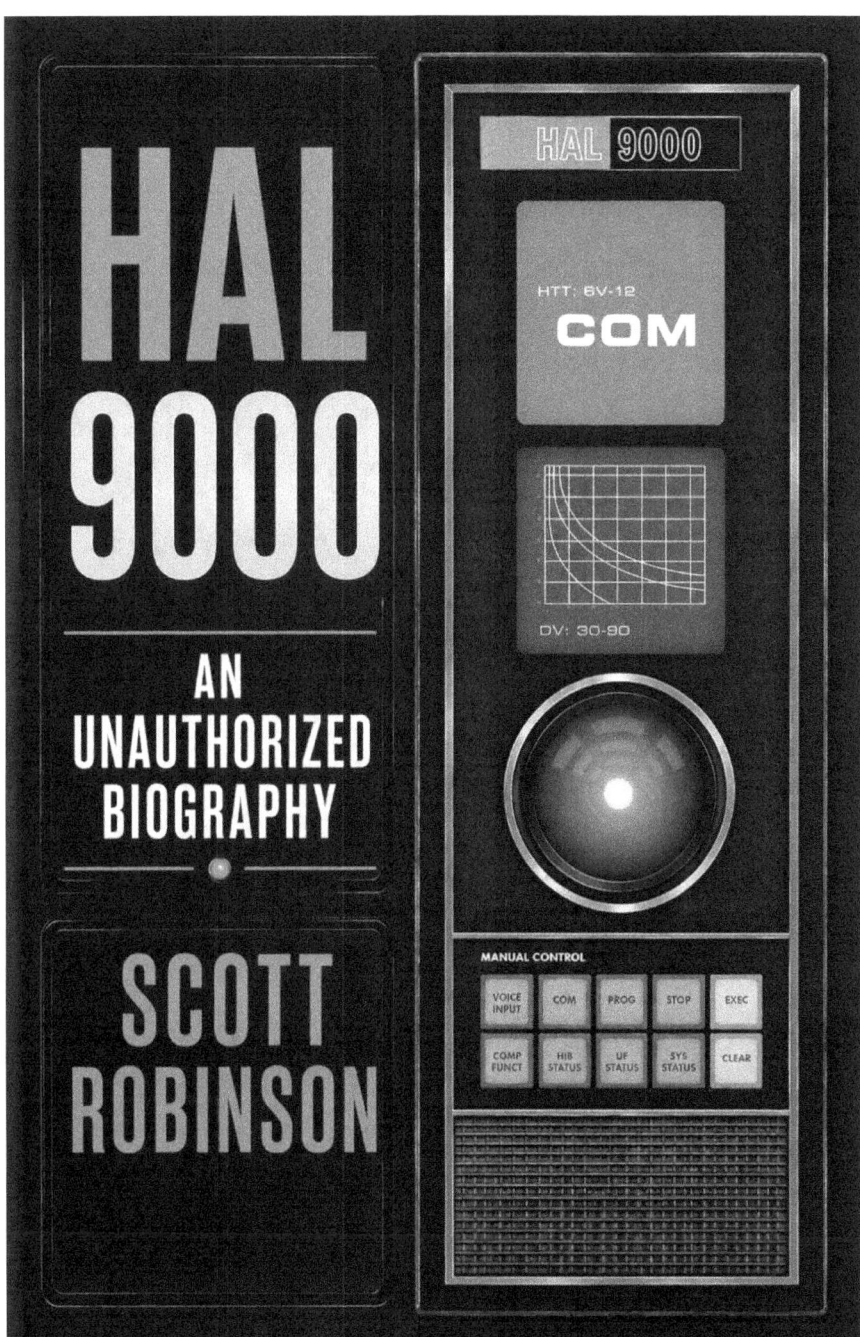

To Everything
That
Might
Have Been

A
Philosophical
Journey

SPACE: 1999

SCOTT ROBINSON

Bibliography / Recommended Reading

The Age of Empathy: Nature's Lessons for a Kinder Society, Frans de Waal. Crown, 2009.

Anatomy of Love, Helen Fisher. W.W. & Company, 2016.

The Authoritarian Specter, Robert Altemeyer. Harvard University Press, 1996.

The Authoritarians, Robert Altemeyer. Internet e-book, 2006.

Behave: The Biology of Humans at Our Best and Worst, Robert Sapolsky. Penguin Press, 2017.

The Better Angels of Our Nature: Why Violence Has Declined, Steven Pinker. Viking, 2011.

The Biology of Moral Systems, Richard D. Alexander. Aldine Transaction, 1987.

Conceiving a Peaceful World: Women's Body Wisdom, Leadership, and Peacemaking, Susan M. Perz. Amazon Digital Services, 2014.

A Cooperative Species: Human Reciprocity and Its Evolution, Samuel Bowles & Herbert Gintis. Princeton University Press, 2011.

The Creation of Inequality, Kent Flannery, Joyce Marcus. Harvard University Press, 2012.

Demonic Males, Richard Wrangham and Dale Peterson. Mariner Books, 1997.

The End of War, John Horgan. McSweeney's Books, 2012.

The Evolution of Cooperation, Robert Axelrod. Basic Books, 2006.

The Evolution of Morality, Richard Joyce. MIT Press, 2006.

Evolutionary Origins of Morality: Cross-Disciplinary Perspectives, Leonard D. Katz (ed.). Imprint Academic, 2002.

Genesis: The Deep Origins of Society, E.O. Wilson. Liveright, 2019.

Hierarchy in the Forest: The Evolution of Egalitarian Behavior, Christopher Boehm. Harvard University Press, 2001.

The Human Potential for Peace: An Anthropological Challenge to Assumptions About War and Violence, Douglas Fry. Oxford University Press, 2006.

Less Than Human: Why We Demean, Enslave, and Exterminate Others. St. Martin's Press, 2011.

Lucy's Courtship: An Integrated Perspective on Human Sexual Evolution, Scott Robinson. Paleos Media, 2011.

The Meaning of Human Existence, Edward O. Wilson. Liveright, 2015.

The Moral Animal: Why We Are the Way We Are, Robert Wright. Vintage Books, 1994.

The Moral Molecule, Paul J. Zak. Transworld Publishers, 2013.

Moral Origins: The Evolution of Virtue, Altruism, and Shame, Christopher Boehm. Basic Books, 2012.

The Most Dangerous Animal: Human Nature and the Origins of War, David Livingstone Smith. St. Martin's Griffin, 2007.

A Natural History of Human Morality, Michael Tomasello. Harvard University Press, 2016.

A Natural History of Peace, ed. Thomas Gregor. Vanderbilt University Press, 1996.

The Neuroscience of Human Relationships, Louis Cozolino. W.W. Norton, 2014.

Non-Zero: The Logic of Human Destiny, Robert Wright. Vintage, 2000.

The Origins of Virtue: Human Instincts and the Evolution of Cooperation, Matt Ridley. Penguin Books, 1998.

Prehistory: The Making of the Human Mind, Colin Renfrew. Modern Library, 2007.

Sapiens, Yuval Noah Harari. Vintage, 2011.

Seducing Ourselves: Understanding Public Denial in a Declining Complex Society, Donna Armstrong. CreateSpace, 2014.

The Selfish Gene, Richard Dawkins. Oxford University Press, 1989.

Social: Why Our Brains Are Wired to Connect, Matthew D. Leiberman. Broadway Books, 2013.

Sociobiology, Edward O. Wilson. Belknap Press, 2000 (25th anniversary edition).

Survival of the Nicest: How Altruism Made Us Human and Why It Pays to Get Along, Stefan Klein. The Experiment, 2014.

The Tangled Wing: Biological Constraints on the Human Spirit, Melvin Konner. Owl Books, 2003.

This Is What I'm Saying, Scott Robinson. Paleos Media, 2017.

Trekonomics: The Economics of Star Trek, Manu Saadia. Pipertext, 2016.

The Triumph of Sociobiology, John Alcock. Oxford University Press, 2001.

Uncle Scott's Treasury of Useless Knowledge, Scott Robinson. Paleos Media, 2011.

Unto Others: The Evolution and Psychology of Unselfish Behavior, Elliott Sober and David Sloan Wilson. Harvard University Press, 1998.

Us Against Them: How Tribalism Affects the Way We Think, Bruce Rozenblit. Transcendent Publications, 2008.

War, Peace, and Human Nature, Douglas Fry (ed.). Oxford University Press, 2013.

Why We Cooperate, Michael Tomasello, et al. MIT Press, 2009.

The World until Yesterday, Jared Diamond. Penguin Books, 2012.

ABOUT THE AUTHOR

Scott Robinson is an artificial intelligence designer, social scientist, public speaker and musician, and serves as Director of Technology and Content for the non-profit Humanity Prime. He has been published in *Rolling Stone* and *The Wall Street Journal*. He can be found at

scottrobinsonwriter@gmail.com

www.ingramcontent.com/pod-product-compliance
Lightning Source LLC
Chambersburg PA
CBHW071341280526
45787CB00001B/176